Big Christianity
What's Right with the Religious Left

Jan G. Linn

Westminster John Knox Press
LOUISVILLE • LONDON

Scripture quotations from the New Revised Standard Version of the Bible are copyright © 1989 by the Division of Christian Education of the National Council of the Churches of Christ in the U.S.A. and are used by permission.

Book design by Sharon Adams
Cover design by designpointinc.com

First edition
Published by Westminster John Knox Press
Louisville, Kentucky

This book is printed on acid-free paper that meets the American National Standards Institute Z39.48 standard. ∞

PRINTED IN THE UNITED STATES OF AMERICA

06 07 08 09 10 11 12 13 14 15—10 9 8 7 6 5 4 3 2 1

Library of Congress Cataloging-in-Publication Data

Linn, Jan.
      Big Christianity : what's right with the religious left / Jan G. Linn.— 1st ed.
         p. cm.
      Includes bibliographical references.
      ISBN-13: 978-0-664-23015-9 (alk. paper)
      ISBN-10: 0-664-23015-6 (alk. paper)
        1. Liberalism—Religious aspects—Christianity.   2. Liberalism (Religion)
      3. Christianity and politics.   4. Religious right.   5. Conservatism—Religious
      aspects—Christianity.   I. Title.

      BR1615.L56 2006
      230'.046—dc22

                                                                    2005058476

This book is dedicated to

Mike Anderson

Marcia Appel

Wally Emerson

Pete Froiland

Vince Giorgi

Judy Grubbs

Kris Koestner

Susan Linscott

Joy Linn

Dirk Niles

CONTENTS

Preface

Mrs. Ann Thiel is eighty-nine years old. She is an inspiring example of the fact that age has nothing to do with whether or not a person continues to grow spiritually. Raised in Christian fundamentalism that continued to be her religious home for many years, she now calls herself a liberal Christian, a label, as we shall discuss, that has fallen out of favor even among liberals. For her, this means believing such things as taxes are the "Christian" thing to do, that homosexuality is nothing to be frightened about, and that setting yourself up as Christian judge, jury, and executioner of others is a fool's game. She wonders whether or not Christians promoting the anti-gay marriage amendments across the country realize the Bible is not much of a guide on "traditional" marriage, given the fact that men in the Bible had children by multiple wives and concubines. She even has questions about the real nature of the relationship between David and his best friend, Jonathan. More than anything, though, she is convinced the Bible is a lot better about telling the truth than a lot of Christians are today.

Mrs. Thiel is a woman after my own heart. Like her, I was raised in fundamentalism and have had to unlearn most of what I was taught about Christianity. My childhood was centered around two- and three-week revivals at my home church where sinners got saved by the dozens. I remember evangelists like Brother Jack Anderson from North Carolina sitting on the top step of the chancel in our church in shirt sleeves, pleading with the congregation to come forward on the invitation hymn and give their lives to Christ. In the parade of preachers I grew up on were singers, artists, and hellfire and damnationers who could put the fear of God in God while leading the congregation in singing, "This is my story, this is my song, praising my Savior all the day long."

None of what I learned in church that I later had to discard to remain a Christian was malevolent. The Christians in my home church believed what they taught me and believed it was what I needed to believe to make my way in the world. I was not traumatized by my experience, only grateful that as a young adult I encountered Christians who understood faith in a different way and encouraged me to join them on a different path.

Mrs. Thiel was not so fortunate. She had to find a new way on her own. Had she simply given up on Christianity, our paths would have never crossed. Sadly, giving up is what many others have done. But she is living proof that there is life after—or other than—fundamentalism.[1]

The irony of my own journey as a recovering fundamentalist is that as a seminary teacher I had the reputation of being somewhat of a conservative. I think that was based primarily on the fact that I wasn't willing to hand Jesus or the Bible over to fundamentalists. The meaning of Christianity was too important to leave in their hand alone, so I decided to put up a fight. This book describes a faith bigger than the small faith I believe fundamentalism has made of Christianity. Though it may not sound like a story, it is an account of the journey people like Mrs. Thiel and myself are on that is leading to an ever-deepening sense that God is bigger than anything we believe and that the appropriate response to this reality is simple humility. That religion has been, and still is, such a divisive force among people is itself testimony to the hubris that infects people of faith. We can be bigger than this, and if we were, the world would be better for it. In these times in which we are living, Christians have a marvelous opportunity to be good-news people. We can be a force for peace, justice, and reconciliation in every land. Differences do not have to become divisions. Instead, they can be woven into a tapestry of religious variety that shows the world that God is good and God is great. My hope is that reading this book will contribute to your wanting to join this journey.

Acknowledgments

*I*t is usual for writers to acknowledge that we are indebted to many people whenever a book has been completed. In this instance, however, that is more true than usual. As I began to write in earnest, I extended an invitation for members of our congregation who wanted to work long and hard to join me in this endeavor. Their role would be to read and critique each chapter, then reread it until I was satisfied we could move on to the next one. As it turned out, that process involved reading all the chapters several times. On top of that, the group members bore responsibility for printing the e-mailed version I sent them each week. This was an unprecedented experience that all of us found awkward at first, as we struggled and learned how to work together in candor and mutual support. But the task was completed with a marvelous celebration of an experience whose significance all of us sensed had transcended the primary work of reading the material. Obviously, I take responsibility for the shortcomings the book may have, but in the truest sense, it is *our* book, not mine. It is a book any member of the group would write. It reflects their faith, their concerns, the issues they care about, and, ultimately, their understanding of what it means to live the Christian life in the modern world. Dedicating the book to them does not adequately express my deep gratitude for having the privilege of serving with them in this wonderful community of faith, but it does provide a modest way to acknowledge their invaluable contribution.

This wonderful group of people is actually a microcosm of the people in the congregation Joy and I are privileged to serve. This is how ministry should be. We confront the serious issues of our time without flinching, and still find a way to enjoy life together. "Fun" may seem an inappropriate word for ministry for the times in which we live, but it seems to capture what it feels like to be in this incredible community of faith.

I am also grateful to all the good people at Westminster John Knox, and, in particular, my editor, Jon Berquist. It was his initiative that gave birth to the book when he wrote to ask, "What are you working on these days?" At the time I had been writing down only the barest thoughts playing around my head. His question and our subsequent conversations became the catalyst for my starting to write in earnest. It is a gift to work with an editor who knows how to balance encouragement and candor.

Finally, my wife, Joy, has believed in the book as much as I have. She not only participated in the reading group, but was as always the person with whom I mulled over sections to make them better. She also graciously supported the hours I devoted to writing that took time away from being together. She even did this on what was supposed to be "vacation." No spouse should endure such a thing. That Joy did without complaint is better than I deserve.

Chapter 1

A Bigger Christianity

Jerry Falwell says mainline Protestant churches have been sidelined and dis-placed by fundamentalist Christianity because our liberal theology is out of step with the American people. There are signs that in this instance his assess-ment is more than political posturing. In March 2005, fundamentalist Chris-tians successfully lobbied the United States Congress to enact legislation on behalf of Terri Schiavo, the brain-damaged woman in Florida whose parents were fighting the right of her husband, Michael, to remove her feeding tube after fifteen years. This was the first time in history a law was passed on the federal level that applied to one person only.[1] In addition, the Republican Sen-ate voted to confirm Christian Right nominees Priscilla Owen, Janice Rogers Brown, and William Pryor to the federal bench as a result of Democrats cav-ing in under the threat of the elimination of the right to filibuster against them. Fundamentalist Christians have also been generally successful in urging Pres-ident Bush to maintain his policy against federal funding of stem-cell research that has promise for finding cures to illnesses such as diabetes, Parkinson's disease, and Alzheimer's disease.

On the state level, constitutional amendments against gay marriage pro-moted by fundamentalists are being approved in several states, such as Arkansas, Georgia, Kentucky, Michigan, Mississippi, Montana, North Dakota, Ohio, Oklahoma, Oregon, and Utah. Even here in traditionally lib-eral Minnesota, polls say that if an amendment goes on the ballot, it will pass by an overwhelming margin.

States are also facing challenges to academic freedom through what fun-damentalists have named the "Academic Bill of Rights." This is a movement started by David Horowitz, a one-time liberal campus activist turned con-servative agitator, for the purported purpose of stemming the tide of liberal bias by college and university professors. The charge is that they are guilty of grading bias and unbalanced, anti-American propaganda. Evidence of

1

such liberal tyranny has been primarily limited to the often-cited statistic that among professors in the humanities and science fields, Democrats outnumber Republicans. The core argument for this Bill of Rights is based upon how conservative students say they feel in classes taught by people they believe to be liberal.

On the face of it, you would think no one would take this kind of thing seriously. On the contrary, the University of North Carolina no longer uses the word "required" in describing the reading program for incoming students about which conservative students lodged a complaint. In Colorado, conservatives withdrew a legislative proposal for an "academic bill of rights" backed by Horowitz, but only after state universities agreed to adopt its principles. Horowitz and backers of the Academic Bill of Rights plan to introduce it in up to twenty other states. Again, in traditionally liberal Minnesota, state Senator Michele Bachmann, a fundamentalist Christian and the primary sponsor of a marriage amendment, has also introduced the Academic Bill of Rights.

Cities and small towns are feeling the effects of the rising tide of Christian fundamentalism as well. Some pharmacists at your local Wal-Mart, Target, CVS, and other stores are refusing to fill prescriptions for birth control and morning-after pills. Karen L. Brauer, president of Pharmacists for Life, which is spearheading this effort, says, "Our group was founded with the idea of returning pharmacy to a healing-only profession. What's been going on is the use of medication to stop human life. That violates the ideal of the Hippocratic oath that medical practitioners should do no harm."[2]

There are dissenters to this justification for the actions of Christian fundamentalist pharmacists, of course. Adam Sonfield of the Alan Guttmacher Institute in New York, which tracks reproductive issues, assesses the situation with the observation, "There are pharmacists who will only give birth control pills to a woman if she's married. There are pharmacists who mistakenly believe contraception is a form of abortion and refuse to provide it to anyone. There are even cases of pharmacists holding prescriptions hostage, where they won't even transfer it to another pharmacy when time is of the essence."

Dissenters or not, pharmacists who let their religious views override their professional conduct are not deterred, and their actions are having serious consequences. As inconvenient as transferring a prescription may be to many people, if you are poor and dependent upon public transportation, the issue is more than a matter of inconvenience. If you happen to live in a small town or a rural area, you may be left without any alternate pharmacy. Moreover, since birth control pills are a hormone and sometimes prescribed for a reason other than birth control, the conscientious objection of a pharmacist becomes even more complicated in its impact on the health as well as the rights of women.

But no matter, fundamentalist Christians are determined to forge ahead in this effort as another front on their antiabortion campaign.

The dominance in the public arena that fundamentalists enjoy today has emboldened them to make some astounding claims. When political commentator George Stephanopoulos asked Pat Robertson if he really believed that "liberal judges" posed "the most serious threat America has faced in nearly four hundred years of history, more serious than al Qaeda, more serious than Nazi Germany and Japan, more serious than the Civil War," Robertson responded, "George, I really believe that."[3]

In similar fashion, a Family Research Council flier promoting its sponsorship of Justice Sunday, a nationwide simulcast program demanding Democrats not filibuster Republican judicial nominees, included the assertion, "The filibuster was once used to protect racial bias, and now it is being used against people of faith."[4] The flier also showed a picture of a teenage boy holding a gavel representing "public service" in one hand and a Bible representing "faith in Christ" in the other. The caption read, "He should not have to choose."

A Christian Right Web site echoed this theme in a posting that said:

> What kind of judges do the liberals want? Those like the ones who allowed Terri Schiavo to be starved and dehydrated to death. Those like the ones who don't believe it should be illegal for abortionists to suck the brains out of nearly-delivered children. Those who believe pornography showing women being raped, mutilated and defecated upon is protected by the First Amendment—but the Ten Commandments are not.[5]

A few weeks after the December 2004 tsunami tragedy in southern Asia that took the lives of more than 250,000 people, Scottish Christian fundamentalist John MacLeod wrote:

> Possibly . . . no event since Noah's flood has caused such loss of life by drowning as the recent Asian tsunami. That so many of our fellow creatures . . . should have perished in so short a time, and in so awful a fashion, was a divine visitation that ought to make men tremble the world over. To rule out the hand of God in this . . . is to forget that He is in sovereign control of all events. . . . If the sparrow falling to the ground is an event noted, and ordered, by Him, how much is this the case when the souls of so many thousands are parted from their bodies?[6]

MacLeod went on to say that "some of the places most affected by the tsunami attracted pleasure-seekers from all over the world. . . . It has to be noted that the wave arrived on the Lord's Day, the day that God has set apart to be observed the world over by a holy resting from all employments and recreations that are lawful on other days. . . . We cannot but fear that it found multitudes unprepared for the eternity into which they were ushered so suddenly and without warning." He said in a later interview, "None of us has reason to be complacent, including myself."[7]

A similar interpretation was given to the devastation caused by hurricane Katrina last year. Michael Marcavage, director of Repent America, a fundamentalist project based in Philadelphia, offered this assessment: ". . . let us not forget that the citizens of New Orleans tolerated and welcomed the wickedness in their city for so long. May this act of God cause us all to think about what we tolerate in our city limits, and bring us trembling before the throne of Almighty God."[8]

But the power of Christian fundamentalism behind the scenes may exceed their public political victories. Though Jerry Falwell is no longer the dominant Christian Right leader he once was, his influence in Washington is still considered significant. But other fundamentalist leaders have emerged whose voices may now be more influential than Falwell's. Fundamentalist pastor Ted Haggard, founder of New Life Church in Colorado Springs, apparently has the ear of many Washington politicians, including the White House, and is widely considered to be the most powerful Christian Right voice in Washington politics.[9]

All of this underscores a new reality wherein liberal Protestant Christians now stand in the shadow of fundamentalism. Our voice in the corridors of power around the country is little more than a whisper. Put bluntly, no one seems to care what liberal Christians think when it comes to matters of morality, values, and politics. A lengthy article in the *New Republic* on religious wars focused exclusively on fundamentalists and evangelicals, with a passing reference to liberal Christians, and then only to note the fact that our numbers are in decline.[10] All signs point to fundamentalism being the dominant religious influence of the early twenty-first century. Falwell, Haggard, Pat Robertson, James Dobson, Ralph Reed, and others close to them have greater influence on the nation's politics and policies than all liberal clergy combined.

This is not to say that fundamentalism has been completely successful in seeing its agenda for America enacted into legislation. Abortion is still legal. Efforts to get a federal constitutional amendment against gay marriage have yet to get much of a hearing, even with a Republican Congress. Formalized prayer in public schools continues to be ruled unconstitutional. Interestingly enough, though it may be the dream of the Christian Right, the political arm of fundamentalism, to see its goals fully realized, its leaders probably understand the observation by sociologist Robert Wuthnow that one of the major factors that dampens any movement is winning. Should the Christian Right achieve its goals, he says, it would have no reason to exist. With every achievement, therefore, its future becomes less bright. Given this reality, Wuthnow says most movements "never really hope to accomplish their stated objectives." He then suggests that for the sake of its future, the Christian Right "will have to pursue the same strategies if it hopes to perpetuate its existence— always champion specific policies, but keep them just beyond reach."[11]

This social reality about the evolution of movements notwithstanding, at the moment Christian fundamentalism is a force to be reckoned with politically. Yet this book intends to show why its moralism and judgmentalism make Christian fundamentalism too small for today's world, a world that is itself both *small and flat*. In his book *The World Is Flat: A Brief History of the Twenty-first Century*,[12] Pulitzer Prize–winning writer Thomas Friedman divides the evolution of the world from size large to size small into three stages. The first period, from the voyage of Christopher Columbus in 1492 to 1800, he calls Globalization 1.0. During this period the world shrank "from a size large to a size medium."[13] What mattered in this era was "brawn—how much muscle, how much horse power, wind power, or, later, steam power— your country had and how creatively you could deploy it."[14] This was a time of global integration.

Next came Globalization 2.0, from 1800 to 2000. This, Friedman says, is when the world shrank "from size medium to size small," driven by multinational companies that went global for markets and labor.[15] Friedman believes that in this period a global economy, fueled by advances in transportation and technology, came of age.

Globalization 3.0 began when the Internet and e-commerce took off around 2003. Friedman underscores how dramatic these developments have been by reminding us that when Bill Clinton was elected to his first term as U.S. president in 1992, virtually no one in or outside government had e-mail.[16] What will distinguish this period from the previous two, he says, is that it will be driven less by American and European individuals than by non-Western groups of individuals, especially in places like India, Japan, and China.[17]

I personally encountered the Globalization 3.0 Friedman describes when I installed a new Lexmark computer printer. My computer was not reading the printer software. Having taught at a seminary in Lexington, Kentucky, for several years, I knew the Lexmark corporate headquarters was there. Calling the toll-free technical assistance line, I was struck by the Indian accent of the technician who picked up my call. As we worked through the problem, I asked him how he liked Lexington, especially the majestic horse farms that circle the city, adding that I had once lived there. "Sir," he said politely, "I am not in Kentucky, I am in Bangalore, India."

But it was not the size of the world that astounded Friedman. It was its shape. Centuries before Friedman traveled to India, Christopher Columbus, who thought he was on the way to India as well, at a time when everyone thought the world was flat, discovered that it was round. In actually reaching India, Friedman discovered that the round world Columbus explored had gone flat. In his own words:

> Columbus reported to his king and queen that the world was round, and he went down in history as the man who first made this discovery. I returned home and shared my discovery with my wife, and in a whisper.
> "Honey," I confided, "I think the world is flat."

The world is both small and flat because technology has leveled the playing field of business and commerce in a way that has made other countries competitive with the United States, especially for jobs. The United States is still a player in the global market, perhaps the major one at the moment. But other nations are now in rapid fashion rightfully claiming a seat at the table.

This small and flat world Friedman describes in his book is a new arena for Christianity that demands a new way of thinking about the role of religion. In a flat world, the playing field has been leveled for all religious traditions. Each is seen as having something to offer people asking questions about the meaning and purpose of life. Christianity is seen as one path, but certainly not the only path leading to God.

In this kind of world, respect for differences becomes a pragmatic necessity, not a distant ideal. Because of its radical exclusivism and sense of religious superiority, Christian fundamentalism is not equipped for this reality. A Bigger Christianity, on the other hand, responds by enlarging its circle as it adapts to a world in which neighbors both real and virtual are diverse in nationalities, cultures, and religions. Even twenty years ago a boy whose family was Hindu was one of our son's best friends in middle school. Today parents from varied national and religious backgrounds sit in the same room at public schools listening to a teacher explain her plans for the new school year. A woman in traditional Muslim dress waits on us at the mall kiosk. The manager of the local supermarket may be a follower of the Dalai Lama. A member of our church says he has benefited immensely from years of practicing Buddhist meditation.

As the inadequacy of Christian fundamentalism to live in the world as it is becomes more apparent, the role of Bigger Christianity will become more important. There are already signs of encouragement in this regard. A few liberal Christian groups have formed in the last few years to counter the impact of the Christian Right, such as the Interfaith Alliance, the Clergy and Laity

Network, Christian Alliance for Progress, and Center for American Progress. While their impact has been modest in comparison to the Christian Coalition, Traditional Values Coalition, and other Christian fundamentalist groups, the fact that such groups have been founded is a positive development.

At the same time, I believe these groups are making a mistake in being reluctant to use the term "liberal" for themselves. They prefer "progressive," as if no one will know you're actually a liberal when you call yourself a "progressive." No wonder, though, since part of fundamentalism's success has been to define "liberal" in such a negative way that the general public believes that it means you don't stand for anything and will fall for everything; that you don't have any principles you stick by, making it impossible for you to have any firm moral foundation for your life. These negative definers of the word actually mean that liberal Christians are not really Christian. If "liberal" as fundamentalists define it is the adjective and "Christian" is the noun, it means a liberal Christian has no principles and morals. No one like this could be a Christian, of course, and that is their point.

It's no surprise liberals are running away from the label. Yet "liberal" is a perfectly wonderful word. The Latin root (*liberalis*, from *liber*) means "free." Since Jesus once said, "You will know the truth, and the truth will make you free" (John 8:32), you would think that "liberal" is an adjective all Christians would want to use to describe themselves. Other meanings are also attractive: "tending to give generously"; "respectful of different people and ideas"; "having or expressing political views that favor civil liberties, democratic reforms, and the use of government power to promote social progress." Aren't these ways that appropriately describe how Christians are to think and act? In point of fact, when you look at the meaning of the word "liberal," it makes you wonder why all Christians don't claim it.

Well, I do. I am a liberal Christian. "Progressive" strikes me as diluting the power of a good word. Besides, it's cleaner just to call yourself what you actually are. Because "liberal" is the adjective and "Christian" is the noun, I am declaring that before I am anything else, I am a Christian, and that is what truly matters. "Liberal" is a description of how I think and act. It is not what I am trying to be. It is *what* I am trying to be that is my primary concern, and that is to be Christian.

Moreover, I believe that being a liberal Christian means you represent the kind of Christianity that is bigger than the small faith of fundamentalism. Sadly, though, because Christian fundamentalism is dominant in the public square, millions of people have become convinced it represents Christianity as a whole. Perhaps that is why so many have left the church. Despite fundamentalist claims of the growth of Christianity, overall church attendance in America has remained flat for the last several years. In part, megachurch growth has been a byproduct of fundamentalists within mainline churches jumping ship. People who are open to a liberal faith are giving up on the church. In his book *Spiritual but Not Religious*, Robert C. Fuller says at least 20 percent of Americans consider themselves "spiritual" but look with suspicion or complete distrust at the church. He quotes one survey that found as many as 54 percent believe "churches and synagogues have lost the real spiritual part of religion," and that one out of three in the survey had reached the conclusion that "people have God within them, so churches aren't really necessary."[18] This development, as Fuller documents, is rooted in the influence of European Enlightenment, which saw numerous efforts among early American leaders like Thomas Paine, Benjamin Franklin, Thomas Jefferson, and later great thinkers such as Emerson and Thoreau to synthesize rationalism and faith.[19]

Admittedly, mainline churches steeped in tradition and resistant to change have also contributed to this situation. But the fact that liberal Christianity is open to questions and not limited by narrow doctrine creates an opportunity for attracting those among the 54 percent who haven't given up on the church completely, as was the case with Kris, a woman in our congregation who a year after joining wrote, "I had, for all practical purposes, given up on the church, convinced that there was no longer a place for me at the Christian table."

Actually, even with our diminished role, the contrast between liberal Christianity and fundamentalism can help draw attention to the bigger faith we represent. Liberal Christians are no better than anyone else in living the faith we claim, but we are not extremists that distort the nation's history and the Christian message to justify a grab for power. We do not believe those who disagree with us are enemies to be vanquished. We have no aspirations to hold prayer meetings in the Capitol rotunda. We are strong in our faith and equally open to non-Christians being strong in their faith or having none at all. We do not believe this is a Christian nation, or that the separation of church and state is a liberal myth. Christian fundamentalism may be mainstream, but that does not change the fact that it represents a religious extremism that all liberal Christians not only disagree with, but choose not to practice.

Fundamentalists want to go back to the 1950s when there was a Christian hegemony in this country. They are determined to undo the gains we as a people have made in accepting religious diversity and building a society of tolerance. The Bigger Christianity you will find pictured in this book does not want to go backwards. It sees the gains in religious tolerance made over the last fifty years as a good thing for the nation and for Christianity, and as a foundation on which to build a better world.

Chapter 2

Framing a Bigger Christianity

*B*igger Christianity represents a fresh framing of the faith needed in a small world, a need that underscores the urgency for liberal Christians to pay more attention to the power and impact of how fundamentalism frames today's important issues. Two weeks before the 2004 presidential election, I was visiting my mother in my hometown of Lynchburg, Virginia. Channel hopping one night, I happened upon the Liberty University cable television channel and the October 17 Thomas Road Baptist Church worship service. Jerry Falwell, beginning what was more a political speech than a sermon, made what I can only describe as an astounding statement: "People say they hate George Bush. Well, let me tell you something. They don't hate him. They hate the Christ in him." At that point the congregation burst into applause. As offensive as the statement was, its appeal lay in the fact that it was framed by the theme "Vote Christian." Falwell indirectly endorsed Republican candidates by identifying what he called "basic Christianity" with the party's positions on abortion, homosexuality, taxes, social security, the war in Iraq, and the appointment of "strict constructionist" Supreme Court justices. Regularly he would insert into his theme the words, "Don't vote Republican. Don't vote Democrat. Vote Christian." But the implication was obvious. Voting "Christian" meant voting Republican.

Liberal Christianity has been unable to gain much traction against fundamentalism in general, or the Christian Right in particular. Part of our problem may be the way in which fundamentalism has been able to frame issues, as Falwell did with his "Vote Christian" mantra. It's time for us to learn how to do some framing of our own, as George Lakoff argues in his book *Don't Think of an Elephant! Know Your Values and Frame the Debate.* A cognitive linguistics scholar, Lakoff suggests the political right has learned how to frame issues to get voters to see the world the way they see it. "Frames," he says, "are mental structures that shape the way we see the world. As a result, they shape the goals we seek, the plans we make, the way we act, and what counts as a good or bad outcome of our actions."[1] He points out that all words evoke "frames." As an elementary exercise, he asks a group of students not to think of an elephant, and, of course, all of them do. They cannot NOT think of an elephant, once he asked them not to. Words create a mental image whether we want them to or not.

In the world of politics, Lakoff says, the goal is to create the mental frame you want voters to have, in order to get them to agree with your position on issues. The right does this effectively, using metaphors and images that create a frame with which people can identify, while often veiling the full intent of what they are advocating. Lakoff cites "tax relief" as one example. Rather than proposing tax cuts for the wealthy, the right calls it "tax relief." It's a frame with which everyone can relate, whether one is wealthy or struggling to make ends meet. "Tax relief" implies getting rid of an unfair burden. Who cannot relate to that? Lakoff further asserts that people vote their identities, which is why "tax relief" is a "frame" that now controls the debate about tax policies. To be against tax cut policies is to be against "tax relief." What is worse, Lakoff points out, is that simply criticizing "tax relief," as liberals do, only reinforces the frame the right has created. Political liberals, he concludes, must learn the art of "framing" issues, if they want to win elections.

One of the persistent weaknesses of liberal Christians is that we who love to use words have not adequately appreciated the power they have to create frames that shape attitudes and behavior. I believe Lakoff would say liberal Christians are like liberal politicians in ignoring the reality that language creates mental images that frame the way people see themselves and the world around them. For too long we have thought that knowledge is power, when in truth knowledge without effective framing is powerless to capture people's imaginations.

If liberal Christians want to offer a version of Christianity that challenges a narrow Christian view of moral values, we will need to learn how to reframe the issues. It is not enough not to be narrow and legalistic as Christians. More important is articulating the kind of Christianity we believe is *bigger* than fundamentalism and its drive to shape the nation's political agenda. The parody below is a stinging comment on the naiveté of liberal Christians in regard to the impact fundamentalism is having on what the American public thinks, and thinks about.

> Liberals made the mistake of thinking that a disastrous war, national bankruptcy, erosion of liberties, corporate takeover of government, environmental destruction, squandering our economic and moral leadership in the world, and systematic political double-speak would be of concern to the electorate.

Fundamentalists correctly saw that the chief concern of the electorate was to keep gay couples from having an abortion.[2]

The importance of how debates are framed is not new. More than a decade ago Robert Wuthnow addressed this need in his assessment of the conflict between fundamentalism and liberalism. Liberal and moderate Christians have allowed fundamentalists to define the agenda, he says, to the point where the former (liberals and moderates) are now reacting to the latter (fundamentalists), rather than vice versa.[3]

> The main challenge facing religious liberals is whether they will continue to let fundamentalists set their agenda for them. Will they continue to serve mainly as a countervoice, offering a haven for those who do not wish to be considered fundamentalists? Will they posture themselves mainly in opposition to the evils of dogmatism and rigidity that they envision in fundamentalism? Or will they in some way be able to rise above the challenge presented from fundamentalism, charting an orthogonal course based on an independent vision of who they are and what they can be?[4]

This is precisely what this book seeks to do in arguing that Bigger Christianity is a new frame for liberal Christians that appeals to people's best instincts rather than exploiting the worst. It feeds on love, not fear. It is a faith for which the words of Jesus have no ambivalence or ambiguity: "By this everyone will know that you are my disciples, if you have love for one another" (John 13:35). It is a faith that trusts love can triumph over fear. It believes that when Jesus unexpectedly came to the disciples walking on water, his words to them were for every generation of Christians: "Do not be afraid" (Mark 6:50). Sadly, fundamentalist Christians are determined to feed the state of fear in which the nation has fallen since 9/11. We are afraid of another terrorist attack. We are afraid of a biological, chemical, or nuclear weapon being set off in a major population area. We are afraid of identity theft. We are afraid of losing our job. We are afraid the moral foundations of the nation are being undermined. We are afraid for our children. We are a people living in fear, consciously or unconsciously. And fear does bad things to people, one of which is to lead them into making very bad decisions and even doing very bad things they would otherwise not do.

A Bigger Christianity does not exploit fear. It seeks to overcome it with an ethic of nonjudgmental love, love without partitions or conditions. It offers people an open circle faith, the bonds of which are made stronger as the circle enlarges. It is a faith that can be fully in the world without being of it. It knows the difference between appeasement and reconciliation, flexibility and unfaithfulness, principle and pride. A Bigger Christianity is never so big as to stand for nothing, nor ever so small as to stand in the way of what God is doing in the world. "Bigger" is not usually better, but when it comes to faith, it is.

Bigger Christianity has no interest in vanquishing enemies, Christianizing America, or promoting a narrow moralism that puts some on pedestals and demonizes others. It works from the conviction that differences do not have to evolve into divisions and that diversity can be embraced without losing one's own identity. It is a faith that lives to love and is willing to risk everything in its service. It is a faith for the peculiar times in which we are living. It is a faith that is strong because it is flexible, particular because it is inclusive, and credible because it makes no claims for absolutism. Bigger Christianity is a faith whose time has come.

But don't take my word for it. More and more prominent Christian voices are beginning to speak on behalf of Bigger Christianity, as did former U.S. Senator John Danforth (R-MO), who is also an ordained Episcopal priest, in an article for the *New York Times:*

> People of faith have the right, and perhaps the obligation, to bring their values to bear in politics. Many conservative Christians approach politics with a certainty that they know God's truth, and that they can advance the kingdom of God through governmental action. So they have developed a political agenda that they believe advances God's kingdom, one that includes efforts to "put God back" into the public square and to pass a constitutional amendment intended to protect marriage from the perceived threat of homosexuality.
>
> Moderate Christians are less certain about when and how our beliefs can be translated into statutory form, not because of a lack of faith in God but because of a healthy acknowledgment of the limitations of human beings. Like conservative Christians, we attend church, read the Bible and say our prayers.
>
> But for us, the only absolute standard of behavior is the commandment to love our neighbors as ourselves. Repeatedly in the Gospels, we find that the Love Commandment takes precedence when it conflicts with laws. We struggle to follow that commandment as we face the realities of everyday living, and we do not agree that our responsibility to live as Christians can be codified by legislators.[5]

Senator Danforth's view represents the kind of Christian left perspective Bigger Christianity can advance. The senator's record in Washington was one that was largely conservative, but not ideological. That is what separates him as a Christian from fundamentalists who are driven by a rigidity that makes religion a sword to be wielded rather than a hand to be extended. Christianity needs a bigger vision of itself and the role it can play in building a world of peace and justice. It is a frame of thinking that fits the small world we rise to meet each day.

Chapter 3

Bigger Christianity as a Voice for God

Who speaks for God in today's small world? Christian fundamentalists believe they do. They consider themselves God's modern-day prophets warning the nation against the evils of liberalism. But are they? How is a person to know?

It is not a new problem. The early church faced the same dilemma. The writer of 1 John cautioned his readers to "test the spirits" to know who is speaking for God and who is not.

> Beloved, do not believe every spirit, but test the spirits to see whether they are from God; for many false prophets have gone out into the world. By this you know the Spirit of God: every spirit that confesses that Jesus Christ has come in the flesh is from God, and every spirit that does not confess Jesus is not from God. And this is the spirit of the antichrist, of which you have heard that it is coming; and now it is already in the world. Little children, you are from God, and have conquered them; for the one who is in you is greater than the one who is in the world. They are from the world; therefore what they say is from the world, and the world listens to them. We are from God. Whoever knows God listens to us, and whoever is not from God does not listen to us. From this we know the spirit of truth and the spirit of error. (1 John 4:1–6)

The text is a warning for Christians to realize there are "false prophets," people who want others to believe they have a message from God when in truth they speak only for themselves. It also indirectly invites caution when claiming to speak for God. But the urgent question it raises is, how do those listening to prophets distinguish between truth and falsehood? Our text boldly provides an answer: "By this you know the Spirit of God: every spirit that confesses that Jesus Christ has come in the flesh is from God, and every spirit that does not confess Jesus is not from God." The letter writer goes on to say that

15

the latter represent "the antichrist" who is already in the world. This is especially curious since fundamentalists say the antichrist has yet to appear. That's a different concern, though. Our focus is the fact that the measure of a true prophet is acknowledging Jesus is from God.

Our text seems obvious enough. But is it? Perhaps acknowledging Jesus is from God isn't as simple as it appears to be. In the Gospel of John, for example, Nicodemus, a Pharisee, comes to Jesus and makes such an acknowledgment: "Rabbi, we know that you are a teacher who has come from God; for no one can do these signs that you do apart from the presence of God" (John 3:2). Instead of applauding him as a "true prophet," Jesus says, "Very truly, I tell you, no one can see the kingdom of God without being born from above" (v. 3). Jesus seems to be saying that acknowledging that he has come from God is not enough. A genuine Christian, and presumably one who speaks for God, must be "born again." This, of course, is Christian fundamentalism language, but the intention may be something quite different from how they use it. The common understanding of being "born again" is that one confesses Jesus as Lord, is baptized in his name, and receives salvation. But Jesus himself says confessing him, that is, being "born again," means much more than this. In the Sermon on the Mount in Matthew's Gospel, he concludes with some very sobering words:

> "Not everyone who says to me, 'Lord, Lord,' will enter the kingdom of heaven, but only the one who does the will of my Father in heaven. On that day many will say to me, 'Lord, Lord, did we not prophesy in your name, and cast out demons in your name, and do many deeds of power in your name?' Then I will declare to them, 'I never knew you; go away from me, you evildoers.'" (Matthew 7:21–23)

The call to be "born again" and the challenge to discern true and false prophecy become more complicated because of this text. Jesus is saying that it is easy enough to confess he is from God with words, but what counts is whether or not the confessor does God's will. That puts us back to square one. What is the will of God? Is it what fundamentalist Christians say it is? Fortunately, Jesus doesn't leave us completely adrift. The sermon itself provides several specific marks of what it means to do the will of God. So in the pursuit of an answer to who speaks for God, it is worth reviewing Jesus' own words as recorded in Matthew's Sermon on the Mount (chapters 5–7). They can be summarized as follows:

Be light (5:14–16)
Seek reconciliation (5:23–24)
Keep commitments you make (5:27–30)

Mean what you say and say what you mean (5:37)
Don't retaliate (5:38–42)
Love your enemies (5:43–45)
Don't show off your faith (6:1)
Know what's important and what's not (6:19–21)
Put God first (6:33)
Measure yourself the way you measure others (7:1–2)
Treat others the way you want to be treated (7:12)

Jesus set the bar high. People who dare to speak on behalf of God's will for today's world, that is, to serve as a prophet, should bring light to any situation. Light dispels darkness, ignorance, prejudice, hatred, bitterness, and on and on. That alone is no small standard to live up to. But they must also model a desire to promote reconciliation between individuals and groups of people. Building barriers rather than bridges is not acceptable. Neither is idolatry. Putting God first in all things has never been easy for people of faith. The church's record is not much better, nor that of any individual Christian I know. We all flirt with idolatry, it seems. A true prophet also keeps commitments made, including, but not limited to, marital vows. Hebrew Scripture refers to Israel's unfaithfulness to covenant with God as "adultery." Sex is not its only context. This is why a prophet's word should be his or her bond. Hidden agendas are forbidden. Trust is the cornerstone for credibility. In addition, prophets do not seek or promote revenge on others. Rather, in attitude, word, and deed they show love and respect for those with whom they disagree. They also treasure that which matters most in life, not least, relationships with others. That is why a true prophet knows judgmentalism is born of pride and is ultimately self-defeating. Above all, true prophets know that how they treat other people demonstrates how they want to be treated.

Clearly acknowledging Jesus is from God means more than belief. Equally clear is that fundamentalist Christians do no better than the rest of us in living out Jesus' call to action, and in more than a few respects do a lot worse. Their words and actions often churn up much heat, but provide little light. Seldom is there a hint of any desire to seek reconciliation. On the contrary, judging others and treating them with disdain seems quite intentional. Moreover, the Golden Rule does not seem to be on their radar screen. Based upon the way we understand Jesus' Sermon on the Mount, we are led to conclude that their version of Christianity is too small to qualify them as true prophets of God.

In point of fact, "smallness" is the primary measure of false prophecy according to the prophetic book of Jeremiah. In chapter 28 the prophet

Hananiah charges Jeremiah with speaking falsely about Judah's future. Rather than the Babylonian captivity of the royal family being proleptic for the nation, Hananiah claimed that within two years God would bring King Jehoiakin (Jeconiah) back to Israel along with the temple's vessels. Jeremiah shouts "Amen!" to Hananiah's prophecy, adding, "May the LORD do so; may the LORD fulfill the words that you have prophesied, and bring back to this place from Babylon the vessels of the house of the LORD, and all the exiles" (28:6). But Jeremiah rejects such talk, causing Hananiah to seize the yoke Jeremiah has placed on his shoulders to symbolize the fate of the nation and break it, declaring the broken yoke as the symbol of God's true actions to come. Jeremiah responds that the broken wooden yoke will be replaced by one made of iron. He then predicts the death of Hananiah within the year. The story ends with the statement that Hananiah in fact died seven months later.

This story states the obvious in regard to discerning true and false prophecy. Whichever prophecy happens is the true one, but this offers little immediate help to a people in need. But there is more in the story than this. Scholars have noted that the two opposing prophets showed very different understandings of God. Hananiah's prophecy rested on the unstated premise that God belonged to Israel. Bound by covenant to protect the nation, God would not allow the royal household and the temple to be destroyed by a pagan power. In contrast, the God of Jeremiah's prophecy was absolutely sovereign over all nations, free to do whatever God chose to do. Jeremiah believed Israel belonged to God. He did not believe that God belonged to Israel. One of the prophets put God in a box, while the other did not. In short, Hananiah's God was too small for Jeremiah.

That is what we believe about Christian fundamentalism. Its faith is too small because it makes the God of creation too small. A liberal faith is bigger, because its message is reconciliation, its method is love, and its goal is the oneness of the human family. A Bigger Christianity believes the Sermon on the Mount is a guide to the behavior the followers of Jesus must try to embody to continue his mission. A Bigger Christianity is the kind of faith that reads the history of the church as primarily an attempt to put God in a box with creeds and dogmas that have caused pain, suffering, and wars, all in the name of Jesus Christ. It believes God is bigger than religion, Jesus is bigger than Christianity, and Christianity is bigger than the church. A Bigger Christianity seeks to show that Christians do not have to be—and should not be—a divisive force in this nation, or in the world. Our faith demands better of us.

This bigger way is for people who reject name-calling as a legitimate means to achieving good ends. It is for people who do not believe being a Christian requires a blanket rejection of the validity of all other religious traditions. A Bigger Christianity is a faith that believes treating others as one wants to be treated *is* the way of Jesus. It believes being a Christian means loving Jesus and loving the way he loved. It believes that living this way is the most effective way there is to be a voice *for* God.

But Bigger Christianity is more than a different attitude. It builds a bigger Christian community. A friend and I were talking about the state of the church when he said in a plaintive tone, "Jan, I just want to be able to go to church with my family. I have one daughter in a biracial marriage. I have two biracial grandchildren. My other daughter is in a committed lesbian relationship. I want a church that will welcome all of us."

This friend and his wife have been active in church all their lives, and very generous with their resources. In most instances they have found a membership far less generous in its attitude toward families like theirs. But there is hope. They have recently joined a new church start that just may have a heart big enough to be the kind of Christian community they need. Such communities do in fact exist in American today. But you have to look for them. You probably won't find them on television, or hear their preacher on the radio. You won't find them occupying a sprawling complex that looks more like a corporate office than a church. No, if you find them at all, they will likely be in a downtown metropolitan area, in neighborhoods most churches abandoned years ago during the height of urban flight. Once in a while you can find one in the suburbs, but it usually turns out to be a new church or a small old one in a modest building without much to make you think it is flourishing. But churches with big hearts do exist.

St. Andrew Christian Church in Overland Park, Kansas, is one, and it is flourishing. Less than twenty years ago it began as a congregation intentionally open to all people, regardless of sexual orientation. The early years were not easy, but today, though it is not a megachurch (and has no desire to be one), its sanctuary is regularly filled with people who claim this open-minded community of faith as their spiritual home. This is a church that would welcome my friend and his family.

There are other churches like St. Andrew. In a 2005 *U.S. News and World Report* article, Diana Butler Bass, a senior researcher at the Virginia Theological Seminary, says there is "a new kind of mainline congregation developing in the United States that's moderate to liberal theologically, taking traditional Christian practices seriously, and is experiencing an unnoticed vitality."[1] As director of the Project on Congregations of Intentional Practice, a three-year study of fifty churches across the country, Bass believes these churches represent a new trend in mainline Protestantism. They're not the most famous congregations in the country, with renowned preachers. In fact, most of them are midsize churches, or smaller. The trend represents at most 6–7 percent of all the mainline churches in the country, but Bass believes the signs are promising and challenge the notion that mainline churches are finished.

At the same time, the fact that you have to look for these kinds of churches says a lot about the state of the church in America today. Numerous are the ones that practice a small Christianity more interested in drawing lines in the sand than circles of care big enough for everybody. There is no lack of churches today whose members attend rallies to support keeping Ten Commandment monuments in courthouses, prayer in public schools, constitutional amendments banning gay marriage, or even conceal-and-carry gun laws. These churches would not welcome my friend and his family. Liberal Christians believe they represent a faith too small to represent the message of love Jesus embodied. It is time for the nation to hear about a bigger alternative. The stakes are high in the current conflict, because the soul of Christianity is hanging in the balance.

Chapter 4

Bigger Christianity for a Small World

*B*igger Christianity *is* a new frame for an old faith. But it needs to get beyond the proverbial abstract to the concrete. As one of my church members said to me the other day, "I don't have any trouble numbering off the things my fundamentalist friends believe, but as a liberal Christian, I can't seem to do the same thing when it comes to what *I* believe." Dirk is not alone. Many liberal Christians know what they don't believe. They're less sure about what they *do* believe. Sometimes it is not even that, though. They know what they believe. They just don't know how to express it, at least in a way that challenges what they were taught growing up in the church as basic Christian beliefs. To address this need, I want to suggest some rather specific ways of thinking and acting that seem to me to embody a liberal faith. Liberal Christians need not be on the defensive when confronted by an unbending and self-confident fundamentalism.

Two convictions are core to everything else we will be saying about Bigger Christianity and represent a huge paradigm shift that will dramatically change the way you think about yourself as a Christian in this small and flat world we occupy. They will open to you a fresh, exciting way of seeing yourself and your relationship to people of other faiths. You will learn why there is no need to insulate your faith from hearing other points of view. These convictions represent a way to live by love, rather than by fear.

The first conviction is that Christianity is more about following Jesus than what you believe about him. Contrary to what fundamentalism says, you don't have to give up on Jesus to be a liberal Christian. Jesus *is* the way for liberal Christians, as he always has been. It's just that now you can focus on being with him, rather than fighting for or against what you believe or someone else believes about him.

In their book on the Lord's Prayer, Stanley Hauerwas and Will Willimon describe Christianity this way:

Think of Christianity, not primarily as a set of doctrines, a volunteer organization, or a list of appropriate behaviors. Think of Christianity as naming a journey of a people. As you read the Gospels, you will note that Jesus and his disciples are always on the way somewhere else, breathlessly on the move. . . .

The journey is an adventure in great part because it is a trip with Jesus, a trip toward trust in him rather than trust in those securities and crutches in which the world has taught us to trust (i.e., bread, bags, and money).[1]

To be a Christian is to have been drafted to be part of an adventure, a journey called God's kingdom. Being part of this adventure frees us from the terrors that would enslave our lives if we were not part of the journey.[2]

In our congregation, "journey" has become a key metaphor for understanding what it means to be a Christian. Recently a small group of adults in our church was discussing marks of spiritual growth I had written about in a previous book.[3] One woman asked, "Aren't these marks the kind of qualities a person of another faith could have as well? If so, why do you call them marks of a *Christian* spirituality? What makes them exclusively Christian?"

It is an important question to which there is a clear answer. No personal quality or action is uniquely or exclusively Christian. Many non-Christians demonstrate personal piety and loving actions that not only equal those of Christians, but may exceed them. History records, and life continues to prove, that Christians have no corner on goodness or good deeds. Bigger Christianity shifts the focus entirely because it believes the *journey* with Jesus is what matters most, not the destination. Its concern is following Jesus, not with heaven and hell, because that is what he asked his disciples to do. He didn't ask them to believe specific doctrines about him. Not even his question, "Who do you say that I am?" (Mark 8:27–30) was posed in a way that suggested it was a key to discipleship. On the contrary, Mark's Gospel says the disciples followed him even though they did not comprehend who he was or what he was telling them.

Jesus said to them, "Why are you talking about having no bread? Do you still not perceive or understand? Are your hearts hardened? Do you have eyes, and fail to see? Do you have ears, and fail to hear? And do you not remember? When I broke the five loaves for the five thousand, how many baskets full of broken pieces did you collect?" They said to him, "Twelve." "And the seven for the four thousand, how many baskets full of broken pieces did you collect?" And they said to him, "Seven." Then he said to them, "Do you not yet understand?" (Mark 8:17–21)

They didn't, of course, but Jesus didn't say they were going to hell for it. Luke says they didn't even understand much about Jesus after the resurrection. The first question they asked had to do with restoring the kingdom of Israel (Acts 1:6). No wonder Mark's story of Peter confessing Jesus as the Messiah says Jesus responded by telling Peter and the others not to say anything to anyone about him (8:27–30). Yet, Peter continued to follow Jesus, and became the first to preach him crucified and raised from the dead (Acts 2:32).

Following Jesus is a journey that leads somewhere. It is not wandering around. It is moving from old ways to new ones, from old loyalties to the only One who is worthy of first devotion. Describing being a Christian as being on a journey is, in essence, to talk about the need of human beings to move from idolatry to faithfulness to God. This is the heart of discipleship. It is less about beliefs than about transformation. That is why the early Christians were called followers of the Way (Acts 9:2). Following Jesus was about a way of living in the world. Today, however, the focus is on believing. Recently new neighbors to one of our children and family expressed surprise and delight in discovering our family members were "believers," in their view the key to the door opening to a good relationship.

This linking of beliefs and relationships is the byproduct of the church defining the meaning of discipleship exclusively in terms of assent to creedal statements. Under pressure from the newly converted Constantine, fourth-century church leaders met at Nicaea and declared in creedal form what one had to believe to be a true Christian, in an effort to end theological controversies that Constantine viewed as a threat to peace in the empire. The Nicene Creed failed in settling the disputes, but along with subsequent creedal statements, it did lead Christians to focus on beliefs about Jesus rather than following him. Indeed, because of what they believed, they often responded to one another in ways that were in marked contrast to the love for one another Jesus said was the primary way the world would know they were his disciples (John 13:34–35). The fact that something was—and is—wrong with this picture has had no impact on Christian fundamentalism. It insists that what matters is who is in and who is out in the eyes of God, and that is determined by what one believes. A non-Christian who lives the way Jesus lived is doomed to "hell" solely on the basis of a failure to believe in Jesus as the Son of God. Further, even those who do believe in Jesus can stand condemned if they do not believe what fundamentalism says they must believe.

This is not the faith of Bigger Christianity. It is less concerned about the "destination" in the hereafter than the transformation here and now. *Big* Christians believe that our identity is defined by the particular journey we have undertaken, which is what is unique for Christians. Jesus is the way to God *for us*. There is no need for a Bigger Christianity to assert that Jesus is the *only* way to God. Fundamentalists say that if Jesus is not the only way, he is no way at all. This is false. *Big* Christians are examples of the fact that one can believe Jesus shows us the way to God and is the human face of God, *and* believe that our faith is not in vain if God has other ways and other faces. Fundamentalism responds that we are not "real" Christians because we don't believe what it says the Bible says we must believe about Jesus, and puts itself in the position of establishing criteria for discipleship Jesus himself did not use. Bigger Christianity rejects the dogma that the validity of Christianity depends upon the invalidity of all other religious traditions. Following Jesus is what makes us Christian, and the validity of Christianity depends on the integrity of our commitment to faithfulness. Moreover, each step on this journey of following Jesus gets us nearer to God and to anyone else who is on a similar journey, regardless of whether they bear the name "Christian" or not.

Big Christians have been on the defensive because we have been too hesitant to say publicly what we believe to be true. We do not have to believe Jesus is the only way to God in order to be one of his followers. Fundamentalism has framed the debate by claiming the name of Jesus without being held accountable for the ways it distorts the life he lived and the message he left with us. The fact is, Bigger Christianity stands tall beside Christian fundamentalism. It is hard to imagine Jesus wanting his church to embody the kind of moralistic legalism he rejected in Judaism. What is more, Bigger Christianity can appeal to people who cannot be fundamentalists, offering instead a faith grounded in following Jesus that celebrates being on the journey with him while leaving the destination in better hands.

The concept of Christian "followship" leads naturally to the second basic conviction of Bigger Christianity—that regardless of circumstances, we can *live out of a sense of abundance*. This is a radical consequence of following Jesus. While material possessions are an element of abundance, they are by no means the sum of it. Living out of a sense of abundance means that the fear of scarcity in a variety of aspects ceases to be a determining factor in your life. But to claim abundant living as Jesus talked about it, the first step is confronting the false promise of American capitalism, which insists the good life is defined by an abundance of things. The dominant culture we rise to every morning does everything in its power to dissuade us from believing we already have abundance.

Common sense tells us money can't buy happiness. But this notion is more than hunch. To a point, money functions in a positive way in providing the means by which people can meet basic needs and satisfy a certain level of wants. But surveys have found that at a variable point based on an individual's intrinsic needs, money begins to have diminishing returns. Conclude the authors of one study,

> Past research . . . has shown that the effect of income on well-being is actually quite strong among those who make less money, because within these people, differences in income translate into differences in how well basic needs are met.
>
> However, further up the income ladder, at the levels where basic needs are satisfied, the effect of income on well-being diminishes.[4]

While Americans experience dissatisfaction when they lack money sufficient to provide for their needs, our happiness quotient does not necessarily rise to match an increase in our bank accounts. In other words, money helps to a point, but in the long run it cannot buy meaning and purpose. Indeed, based on findings in another study led by David Blanchflower, a professor of economics at Dartmouth College, researchers concluded, "The problem we have found is that as [gross domestic product] has gone up, happiness doesn't go up with it."[5] Further, based on interviews of 100,000 people over three decades, they found that that despite sharp improvements in living standards "the United States has, in aggregate, apparently become more miserable over the last quarter of a century."

So why do so many people continue to chase after money? What motivates Americans to pursue happiness through material possessions when the data says money cannot live up to its claims? As surveys indicate, the answer varies with individuals, but in general it comes down to the fact that most Americans still buy into the illusion that more is better. Moreover, that widespread notion is born of a naiveté that says you can never have too much of a good thing.

Nothing could be further from reality. Think about blood cells for a minute. A single drop of blood contains millions of red cells that are constantly traveling through the body delivering oxygen and removing waste. If they weren't, our bodies would slowly die. White blood cells are no less important, as they fight infections and diseases. Red and white cells work together. They are good things to have. But when the body starts producing more than it needs of either one, it has too much of a good thing.

Money is a good thing. It can do enormous good. It is a means to many noble ends. But we can also have too much of this good thing, though most of us don't believe it. The divide separating want and need is thin. Because money buys things, when we can buy anything we want, it is easy to believe we never have enough of what we need. Yet one thing money cannot buy but we always need is the ability to see what it does to us when we have too much of it.

Our culture, of course, has convinced us that we can never have too much money. It's the key that unlocks the door to independence, an American value second only to the money that most people believe buys it. The irony is that most of us never feel as if we have enough of what we have been conditioned to think we can never have too much of, because we are suffering from *affluenza*, [6] a disease whose primary symptom is an insatiable desire for more. *Affluenza* thrives on runaway materialism by convincing people that the good life consists of financial independence. The multimillion-dollar American advertising industry has one goal: to convince the buying public that happiness does in fact consist in the abundance of things.

We are susceptible to this lie because our materialistic culture has co-opted the true meaning of abundance. I personally made this discovery three years ago, not long after I had given up a tenured seminary position to join my wife as copastor of a new church start. I was on the phone describing our struggles as a new congregation to keep our head above water to a longtime friend named Judith, who is a therapist by profession. In some detail I told her about the issues we were confronting and our longing for the day when we would not have to wonder if we were going to make it financially. Judith listened, and then when I was finished, she gently said, "Now, Jan, I want to invite you to live out of your abundance."

I remember being silenced by her comment, thinking perhaps the cell phone connection had been lost while I was talking, so I summarized what I had spent ten minutes telling her. She replied she had heard me the first time and then repeated her invitation: "I want you to live out of your abundance." The only thing I could think to say in response was the obvious: "Well, I'm not sure I understand what you mean about abundance. We don't seem to have any."

"Well," she replied, "You just told me that even with your struggles, you were keeping your head above water. So you have enough for today. That's abundance, and I invite you to live out of that rather than worrying about what you don't have or dreaming of the day when you won't have to."

That phone call began an ongoing conversation that has turned my thinking upside down. As if a light bulb had been turned on in my head, I realized that I had always thought of abundance as having "enough and to spare," when in reality it simply means having enough. Further, "enough and to spare" thinking creates the mindset wherein when "the spare" begins to dwindle, there is an immediate anxiety about the "enough." That in turn produces a need to take steps to protect it, making possessiveness appear to be a reasonable response to diminishing resources. But as anxiety over the enough rises, distinguishing between need and want becomes very difficult.

As I look back over my life, I have hardly ever had a genuine reason to be anxious about not having what I needed. In reality, financial anxiety has been much more related to what I have wanted than to any real need. Many people do not have what they need, but I am not one of them. I have often found myself worrying about money, that good thing I can never have too much of, when I had enough of it at that moment. Thus, living out of abundance was not how I would have ever described my life.

Yet Scripture boldly affirms abundance as "having enough" and rejects out of hand the notion that it means "enough and to spare." Manna in the wilderness, for example, had to be collected fresh every morning (Exodus 16:15–36). The people received unequivocal instructions. Nothing was to be saved or stored up. When the people ignored what they were told, they discovered the "manna" had spoiled. Enough for the day was abundance. Trying to secure "enough and to spare" put the "enough" in jeopardy.

Jesus restated this wisdom when he cautioned against worrying about having basic needs tomorrow.

> "Therefore do not worry, saying, 'What will we eat?' or 'What will we drink?' or 'What will we wear?' For it is the Gentiles who strive for all these things; and indeed your heavenly Father knows that you need all these things. But strive first for the kingdom of God and his righteousness, and all these things will be given to you as well." (Matthew 6:31–33)

He also said, "Take care! Be on your guard against all kinds of greed; for one's life does not consist in the abundance of possessions" (Luke 12:15). The apostle Paul wrote, "And God is able to provide you with every blessing in abundance, so that by always having enough of everything, you may share abundantly in every good work" (2 Corinthians 9:8). He further declared that he had learned how to be content whether in times of plenty or times of want (Philippians 4:10–12).

None of these texts suggests there is no need for concern over basic necessities or justifies lack of compassion for those who do not have them. They simply highlight the inherent tension between need and want, and how difficult it is to attend to the former without being consumed by the latter. Neither do these passages argue for a "blind trust" in God to provide for basic needs without human effort or responsible decision making. Rather, they offer a practical guide for living in a material world without becoming "of" it. Abundant living consists of having enough for today. We do not know about tomorrow, and yesterday is gone. What matters is having enough today.

Living out of abundance is core to Bigger Christianity, because it removes the need to "be against" another faith tradition in order to "be Christian." Jesus said as much:

"No good tree bears bad fruit, nor again does a bad tree bear good fruit; for each tree is known by its own fruit. Figs are not gathered from thorns, nor are grapes picked from a bramble bush. The good person out of the good treasure of the heart produces good, and the evil person out of evil treasure produces evil; for it is out of the abundance of the heart that the mouth speaks." (Luke 6:43–45)

The heart filled with a sense of abundance speaks the language of love. Wherever that language is spoken, bridges are built between people whose differences are real. This happens because living from abundance takes the "one day at a time" philosophy and applies it to the whole of life. Obviously it strikes against the power of money to seduce us, but it also guides our emotional, psychological, and mental selves. In other words, abundance consists of more than money, and extends to love, relationships, self-confidence, job satisfaction, setting and achieving personal goals, and many other concerns. Love, in fact, is the quintessential symbol of living out of abundance. The less we try to possess love, the more we have of it. There is no anxiety over sharing it because our daily experience confirms and reconfirms that having enough for today is in fact to have it in abundance. What is true about love applies to all aspects of our lives.

It is easy to see how generosity freely flows from living out of abundance. When it depends on the "to spare" in our lives, generosity becomes mercurial, as our sense of plenty and scarcity goes up and down. In a good year we are very generous. In a bad year we cut back. Having enough is not enough because the leftovers are dwindling. Which means those being fed from table crumbs are likely to get less and less when there is a "spare crumbs" shortage. But living out of abundance takes "scarcity" out of the equation. So long as there is enough for today, there is no such thing as scarcity. There is only abundance.

Abundance means economic status has no effect on whether or not we live out of it. Jesus' words that it is possible to live without worrying about tomorrow do not depend upon the size of one's portfolio. This is why his gospel is both revolutionary and comforting. Turning the world upside down has to do with the way Christians can live without fear and want in the face of having nothing but enough to get through the day. Recently a woman in our church told the story of listening to a conversation between her husband and his cousin about immigration. They were strong in their opposition to letting so many "aliens" come into the country taking jobs away from Americans. From their perspective, this country couldn't afford to keep letting this happen. Bothered by the conversation, but not saying anything at the time, the next day this woman decided to tell her husband she needed him to know she was upset by the conversation because she believed his attitude about immigration contradicted what they had been hearing at church about living out of abundance. His first response was to become defensive, but a day later, with tears in his eyes, he apologized, saying he realized she was right about living out of abundance.

The apostle Paul tells us of some churches whose members understood what this couple was discovering. Writing to the Corinthian Christians, he commends to them the example of the churches of Macedonia.

> We want you to know, brothers and sisters, about the grace of God that has been granted to the churches of Macedonia; for during a severe ordeal of affliction, their abundant joy and their extreme poverty have overflowed in a wealth of generosity on their part. For, as I can testify, they voluntarily gave according to their means, and even beyond their means, begging us earnestly for the privilege of sharing in this ministry to the saints—and this, not merely as we expected. (2 Corinthians 8:1–5)

Abundant joy filled the minds and hearts of these Macedonian Christians, despite their poverty and difficulties. This abundance had expressed itself in a generosity Paul believed exceeded that of the Corinthians in providing financial support to the Jerusalem church.[7] In citing the Macedonian churches as an example to follow, Paul was urging the Corinthians to do what a friend refers to as "leading with generosity." The Macedonians had a strong sense of abundant joy, but the Corinthians didn't have to wait to have it. If they led with their generosity by following the example set for them, they would experience abundance. Abundance produces generosity. Generosity produces abundance.

This is the way of Bigger Christianity. It is the practical face of the biblical concept of being "born again." Liberal Christians have allowed fundamentalism to co-opt this powerful phrase Jesus spoke to the Pharisee, Nicodemus, who came by night to ask him if he was truly the one for whom the Jews had been waiting (John 3:3). Jesus told Nicodemus that seeing the work of God requires the eyes of one who had been "born again." But the text does not support interpreting this as an assurance of "going to heaven." Instead, experiencing a daily abundance that guides the way you live in the here and now is a more likely understanding of the meaning of his words for today. Living out of abundance has an immediate and at the same time nascent effect on one's life. It is a present and at the same time "not yet" experience of learning how to be content in all circumstances. Circumstances do matter. It would be naive or callous to think they don't. The point is that abundance as "enough" is the key to a freedom that is not subject to external pressure or control. It may actually be the truth Jesus said would set us free (John 8:32).

Sam Jones is a businessman who will tell you about living out of abundance. Having spent several years living on the high end of sales commissions, he made the decision to start his own company and get out from under the pressure of working for someone else. Three years into it, he was over his head in debt, having gone from being able to buy anything to being unable to pay for what little he had left. His is the story of going from riches to rags. But along the way he learned about living out of abundance. Today he will tell you it has changed and is changing his life. He sleeps better, lives with less stress and anxiety, and is at peace with himself. Yet very little externally would suggest he could live this way. After all, he has quite literally lost everything he once worked so hard to acquire. But Sam says life is good because he has enough for today. He describes his life as having abundance unlike any he has ever known.

This is not the kind of story that makes Wall Street news, but it reflects how the truth about abundance does change life. Sam hopes tomorrow will finally begin to show a turnaround in his efforts to put his company on the road to financial success. But his peace of mind and self-esteem don't depend on it. He is successful as a man, husband, father, church member. He just wants his business to catch up with him.

Sam's story exposes the lie of unbridled American capitalism, which claims without apology or shame that life does consist in the abundance of things. This is what drives the American economy. Yet Christian fundamentalism believes what is good for America is good, period. Consequently, it sees *affluenza* as a problem of personal moral weakness. Capitalism itself cannot be the issue. The concern about systemic injustices is the creation of liberals who want to destroy the American way of life.

This blind support of unregulated capitalism is rooted in fundamentalism's triumphalism, which asserts the God who chose Israel as a covenant partner has now chosen America to be the light of the world. To acknowledge systemic problems inherent in the American way of life in general—and American capitalism in particular—would reflect badly on God. The problem is not the system. It is the individuals in it. Within this framework, *affluenza* is nothing more than a byproduct of individual disobedience and/or irresponsibility. The system itself bears the blessing of God and cannot be flawed.

The way fundamentalism describes the relationship between God and country connects with many Americans, because it Americanizes God and presupposes a divine blessing that sets America apart from other nations. Patriotism and godliness become two sides of the same coin. Throw in the American dream of economic success, and capitalism becomes a God-inspired system of rewarding those who honor God with hard work. The playing field is America, and, thus, always level.

Abundance, on the other hand, is a perspective balanced with gratitude and generosity. Free enterprise that produces "enough and to spare" is not the enemy, but neither is it baptized as if uniquely blessed by God. Seen as a human system without divine sanction or endorsement, it needs to be subjected to regular examination, to ensure that it is not controlled by the few at the expense of the many. In addition, money is seen for what it is, a means to an end, not an end in itself. It is a tool of exchange that allows society to function. Being wealthy in and of itself is not to be praised or derided. The task is always to remember that in the scheme of things, having enough of what money buys is enough. There is no need to hoard it or be possessive of it. Christians who have more than they need must "keep their head"[8] economically, even if some around them are losing theirs. Living out of abundance is not a bare-necessities kind of existence—quite the opposite, in fact. Having enough means focusing on the gifts of the day without spoiling them in the desire for more.

At any time "enough and to spare" can ruin the "enough." The tax revolt across the nation is an example of how this happens. Initiated and fueled by a coalition of wealthy and middle-class Americans who want for nothing, this "revolt" preaches that taxes rob people of their God-given right to acquire more. The issue is not about needs. Members of taxpayer leagues make a comfortable living. What they do lack is a sense of abundance that spawns a generosity supporting the common good. The current "war" on taxation not only threatens the social bond that free nations must have to prosper; it stems from the conviction that abundance means having more. It is not surprising that the people who pressure politicians to sign no-new-tax pledges believe that because this is America, where the pursuit of "more" is open to all, anyone willing to work hard can have it. Family history, early childhood circumstances, educational opportunities, race or nationality, cultural influences— none of these matter. God helps those who help themselves.

Bigger Christianity rejects this Benjamin Franklin view of God. It supports policies consistent with the impulse for human connectedness that it believes is born of God. Rather than having a blind trust in the power of trickle-down economics, it works to direct the power of private and public resources to social problems. Bigger Christianity does not need to be convinced there are Americans who are victims of corporate and government behavior that literally puts their lives at risk. It understands that generosity can be abused, but it also understands that the real problem in this country is not laziness, but *affluenza*. Bigger Christianity, therefore, rejects American triumphalism, which serves as a de facto theological justification for this disease.

Abundant living is the way of a *big* faith and serves as the foundation upon which Christians can build a better world. This better world is our goal. Because *big* Christians embody this kind of Christian faith, we cannot be content to work for a better life just for ourselves. Our personal well-being is bound to that of the whole human family. Nor is guilt the motivation for caring about the common good. Rather, it is generosity spawned by living from the abundance of having enough for today. Giving out of abundance because there is no anxiety about not having enough is as natural as breathing.

One of Jesus' most instructive stories is about the man who built new barns to contain excess grain (Luke 12:16–21). As the story goes, the land produced "abundantly." Unable to store all of it safely, he tore down his old barns and built new, larger ones. Satisfied with his decision, his soul was content. But tomorrow was not to be his. The man who had enough for the day died in the pursuit of even more.

In its Gospel context, the story is a warning about being rich in the wrong things. But it speaks with equal force to remind us today that part of the "wrong things" is seeking an overabundance of the good things in life, and in the process missing the abundance right in front of us. The kind of Christianity we are describing is wise enough to know there is, indeed, such a thing as too much of a good thing.

The two core convictions of *followship* and *abundance,* then, define Bigger Christianity as following Jesus into abundant living. That is the whole thing in one sentence. Followship doesn't mean that what you believe about Jesus is unimportant, only that you can follow him whatever you believe or if you are not sure what you believe about him. This is because the journey is about learning how to live out of your daily abundance. This frees you from being consumed by a sense of scarcity that can make you anxious and fearful, whether it be about money or love or faith. As this happens, you begin to embrace ways of thinking and acting that not only change you, but can change the world.

Chapter 5

Embracing Bigger Christianity

*E*ven if thinking about Christianity as a journey defined by abundant living appeals to you, it will take on real meaning only as you begin to make specific choices between a big Christianity and a small Christianity. These choices will be easier for some than for others. My fundamentalist background has made my journey to abundant living slower than it has been for others. Being a liberal Christian does not mean any of us is better than fundamentalists at making hard choices. Emotional, spiritual, and ego needs influence our decisions as much as they influence theirs. But on the whole, we can make choices that deepen our commitment to staying on the journey and resisting the temptation to live by a sense of scarcity rather than abundance.

One of the gifts of life is the ability to choose how well we live. We are tempted to believe we do not control our lives, but at the most basic level, we do. Nelson Mandela, the former president of South Africa and perhaps the greatest political leader of the twentieth century, exemplifies this fact. Mr. Mandela spent twenty-seven of the best years of his life in prison unjustly. When he walked out of the Robben Island prison on February 11, 1990, he resumed his work to build a nation in which all citizens would enjoy freedom and justice, doing so as if the intervening years in prison had not happened. His autobiography, *Long Walk to Freedom*,[1] makes it clear that picking up where he left off was a *choice*. He could have made other choices that reflected justified anger and bitterness. He chose the road less traveled.

His was a magnificent choice, but it was a choice like all the choices we make daily. Choices are the opportunity life gives us to be cocreators with God. In some instances they represent forks in the road. At other times, they seem more like a crossroads. In every instance, though, they offer a chance for us to make something of ourselves and/or have an impact on the lives of others. There are no unimportant choices when it comes to determining the quality of life for anyone. It may be a bit presumptuous to put the choices below in this lofty category. At the same time, they do describe decisions that will determine whether or not we embrace a Bigger Christianity that can make a positive contribution to the small and flat world in which we now live.

People of God Alone vs. The Only People of God

On summer evenings the Athenaeum Hotel on the grounds of the Chautauqua Institution serves dessert on the grand porch that looks out over Chautauqua Lake. Chautauqua is one of the very special places in the world, founded in 1874 by Lewis Miller, an Akron, Ohio, inventor and manufacturer, and John Heyl Vincent, a Methodist minister, who later became a bishop. Its guiding principle has been from the beginning the belief that every person "has a right to be all that he can be—to know all that he can know." Today its summer program of study, learning, and recreation draws thousands of visitors from many countries and different faith traditions. It was a Tuesday when my wife, Joy, and I walked down to the hotel to enjoy this special experience. Upon arrival, we noticed Mohamed Keshavjee, one of the guest lecturers for the week sponsored by the department of religion, sitting at a table in the dining room with two of his colleagues. Serving as chaplain of the week, we had become acquainted with the three Muslim men in conversations around the breakfast table at the Hall of Missions, where all of us were being housed. It had not taken long for the group of us to discover that as Christians and Muslims we shared a common commitment to religious tolerance.

We told these new friends that we had come down to the hotel to enjoy dessert on the porch and invited them to join us after their meal. They suggested we first join them. We agreed, and began a conversation that lasted into the night. We talked about Islam, Christianity, the Israeli/Palestinian conflict, the image of America in the Muslim world, the image of the Muslim world in America, and much more. These men spoke from the depths of their Muslim faith in ways that paralleled our own Christian convictions. It was one of those fortuitous—or providential—moments one cannot plan or anticipate that has a lasting impact on your life. As we walked back to the Hall of Missions and retired to our rooms, Joy and I both knew this time had been a special experience of making connections as members of the human family at a deep level.

This was not the first time I had experienced the bond of our common humanity. During my years of teaching and serving as chaplain at Lynchburg College in Virginia, a small, church-related liberal arts college, Rabbi Morris Shapiro taught me to read Hebrew. That began a relationship that evolved into a treasured friendship. On several occasions I invited Morris to preach at chapel. He graciously invited me to preach at Friday evening Sabbath service. When he and his family celebrated the Seder meal at synagogue for people without immediate family in the area, he invited me to join in the celebration. It forever changed my understanding of the Lord's Supper. Looking back, I am confident he felt as I did—that our relationship both highlighted and transcended our different backgrounds and faith traditions.

These experiences, separated only by the years, confirmed what I had known to be true before they occurred. I am a Christian who cannot presume to be loved by God at the expense of others who are of another religious tradition. The God of my faith cannot reject people of differing faiths from covenant because they do not believe in Jesus as "Lord and Savior." Rather, it seems so obviously Christlike to accept them as people of faith with whom Christians share life as the *b'nai b'rith*—the children of covenant. I cannot conceive of a God whose heart is smaller than my own. If others do, that is both sad and tragic, but it is no reason to follow their example. I can no longer listen to voices that in tone and content bear little resemblance to what I read in Scripture. If Jesus was the human face of God, as I believe he was, then love, grace, and forgiveness multiplied seventy times seven define the context for God's claim on our loyalty. Making divine grace exclusively Christian makes Christianity too small.

The sign standing outside our church building includes the words "A Community of Open Minds and Open Hearts." It's the kind of church we are seeking to be. As a new church, we need everyone who walks through the door—but, we have learned, not at any price. We are a new congregation whose identity is mainline Christian. For us this means being a church that doesn't have all the answers. No church does, of course. We just happen to be willing to admit it. That is why we treasure an open mind. When you know you don't have all the answers, you want to learn, you want to be free to let your mind and heart wander where either desires to go. Ours is a congregation that resists dogmatic statements of faith. Were we to vote on it, we would affirm Eckhart Tolle's assessment:

> Dogmas—religious, political, scientific—arise out of the erroneous belief that thought can encapsulate reality or truth. Dogmas are collective prisons. And the strange thing is that people love their prison cells because they give them a sense of security and a false sense of "I know."[2]

Tolle may have overstated the case when he says, "nothing has inflicted more suffering on humanity than its dogma,"[3] but more than a few of our members have learned through experience "that every dogma crumbles sooner or later, because reality will eventually disclose its falseness; however, unless the basic delusion of it is seen for what it is, it will be replaced by others."[4] Thus, our church believes that the desire to learn is basic to being a disciple, a student, a follower. In addition, one of the truly joyous experiences a Christian can have is to be in a community of faith where questions are welcomed and no one is judged unworthy based on theological nonconformity.

Bigger Christianity forms this kind of community, one in which Christians not only explore their own faith, but are willing to learn how to be Christian in a religiously plural world. Bigger Christianity is unafraid to think that God works in and through a multitude of faith traditions. That is why it is a faith for the times in which we live. Religious pluralism is a historical reality that cannot be ignored. This is especially the case for American Christians. In her seminal work *A New Religious America*, Diana Eck underscores the fact that not only have the massive movements of people both as migrants and refugees reshaped the demography of our world into a new geo-religious reality,[5] but "nowhere . . . is the sheer range of religious faith as wide as it is today in the United States."[6] It seems an understatement for her to add, "We have never been here before."[7]

Nor are we necessarily equipped to cope with this reality. In truth, Americans are not as tolerant as we think we are. Nor have we ever been. The truth about America, Eck's book documents, is that from the beginning our nation has had both religious diversity, albeit Christian, and conflict because of it. Despite public declarations of tolerance, we have not practiced what we preached.

> Religious freedom and what today is called religious pluralism have not always been the American way, even though they have now become an integral part of the story of our country. History reminds us, however, that widespread religious freedom was hard won in this land, and disagreement about how to handle religious differences is as old as the American experiment.[8]

In light of the rise of Christian fundamentalism's influence in American politics, nonfundamentalists ought to be asking ourselves if that movement is promoting a culture of intolerance that will fuel the fires of religious conflict. Fundamentalism insists that tolerance has become another name for permissiveness. This kind of thinking easily slips into an attitude of exclusion. Eck says that in early America, this amounted to closing the door on immigration in order to keep out those who were creating too much diversity.[9] Today we are not only closing the door, but putting motion detectors on the ankles of all immigrants whose status is under investigation,[10] with strong support for this practice from fundamentalist Christians who believe immigration is a problem for which exclusion is the solution.

We might be encouraged that a few fundamentalist Christians support the freedom of members of other faith traditions to practice what they believe freely as an example of American democracy. Unfortunately, what they actually mean is that people of other faiths can worship freely as long as they understand this is a Christian nation. Eck calls this the "assimilation" approach to religious diversity that basically says, "Come and be like us."[11]

Bigger Christianity is a better alternative for how Christians can live in the world of today, because it can thrive in the context of religious pluralism. Using the words of Eck, its attitude is, "Come as you are, with all your differences, pledged only to the common civic demands of citizenship. In other words, come and be yourselves."[12] This is the attitude most consistent with a nonfundamentalist reading of the Bible and offers a viable and powerful alternative to Christian fundamentalism. It also serves as the foundation for calling together a coalition of various religious traditions to form a *real* religious left, as we explore in detail in chapter 7.

In affirming the reality of religious pluralism, Bigger Christianity is not a compromised faith, as fundamentalism would claim. It is, rather, an informed faith that rejects the dogmatism of the past, which, by promoting intolerance of others, has limited our vision of how to be faithful to what we believe. I have met numerous Christians who do not like fundamentalism, but seem unaware of how to be a Christian any other way. Unfortunately, as a result a lot of these people have abandoned the church, opting for freedom to chart their own journey of faith without the church's interference. In fact, the "dechurching" of Christianity may be the price we are paying for the dominance of fundamentalism today. Clergy usually stay around to fight theological battles, but increasingly lay people are deciding it's not worth it. And not just the young. Seniors are also dropping out of church.

What is ironic is that Bigger Christianity is open to other religious traditions precisely because it is so Christian. We are not pluralistic *in spite of* being Christian. *We are pluralistic because we are Christian.* We trust that the heart of God is larger than our own. We trust that the love of God is more accepting than our own. We trust that the truth of God is more profound than anything we can understand. We believe Jesus' table is large enough for all the sons and daughters of Abraham to sit down and share together. Bigger Christianity believes an open table in an open circle expresses the hope of those who honestly pray, "Your kingdom come; your will be done, on earth as in heaven."

Pluralism is an enemy of Christianity only to those whose God lives in a box or a temple or a church, rather than in the whole of creation. Jesus is the way, the truth, and the life for Bigger Christianity. This confession means we are willing to listen to Jesus, the Jesus who said, "Whoever does the will of

God is my brother and sister and mother" (Mark 3:34). That is a very big family, bigger than the small Christianity of fundamentalism. That is why, as liberal Christians, we seek to have a big faith in this small world in which we are privileged to live.

Inclusion vs. Exclusion

Being Christian means being on a journey with Jesus, whose circle of relationships is larger than Christians tend to imagine. So it is difficult to understand why fundamentalists believe "inclusiveness" means being permissive—means excluding nothing, because you have no standards. Ironically, the verb "include" actually underscores just the opposite. When we say something "includes" this or that, we mean that some elements are left out. By implication, therefore, a community that is inclusive is not one that has no standards and makes no assessment of what is needed and not needed. Quite the opposite, inclusion means seeking precisely what is needed to make something complete or whole, leaving out what would not contribute to this end. Thus, the church practices inclusion by welcoming all who want to share in the hard work of moving from idolatry to faithfulness.

The verb "exclude," on the other hand, points to a desire to shut out something or someone. It even means to fail to notice, choosing instead to disregard. For Christians to be "inclusive" rather than "exclusive" means taking positive action to promote faithfulness on the broadest scale possible, rather than aggressively limiting access to such faithfulness by using arbitrary standards that often end up becoming idolatrous themselves. Jesus' focus was on "inclusion." The Gospels portray him as reaching out to a variety of people, as if including them was essential to the welfare of the whole. But his actions stand in contradistinction to other religious leaders who aggressively excluded the very people Jesus included. It is astounding that some Christians today are acting just like those who opposed Jesus, but doing it in his name. Bigger Christianity believes in the power of inclusion. We do not fear differences. We do not consider diversity an enemy of faith. Rather, we think of it as the means of making the whole in fact *whole*.

One well-known example of Jesus' ministry of inclusion is the adulterous woman whom the Pharisees wanted to stone to death (John 7:53–8:11). The contrast between their attitude toward her and Jesus' attitude underscores what we are saying. They acted out of legalism, because their focus was moral purity. That in turn led to an emphasis on exclusion as a means of enforcing purity as they understood it. Jesus, on the other hand, focused on people, which led him to an emphasis on relationships. Inclusion was the means to this end. For the people listening to Jesus that day, it was not a matter of realizing he was right and the Pharisees were wrong. If anything, their first inclination would have been to side with the Pharisees. What must have struck them, therefore, was the fact that Jesus focused on the woman rather than the law. He didn't disregard the law. He simply made it an instrument to a greater end, not an end in itself. The message they heard in his actions was that the circle of law naturally excludes, while the circle of Jesus' love naturally includes.

Bigger Christianity affirms inclusion as the standard by which Jesus wants his followers to relate to all people and all other religious traditions. The larger the circle, the richer the whole becomes. This is why we do not understand why fundamentalist Christians want to play the role of judges who determine who can be in the circle and who must stay outside. They, of course, say they are not judging, just following the Bible. But as the story above illustrates, they do not seem bothered by texts about Jesus' acting or speaking in ways that contradict how they act and speak. My own experience has been that no one is diminished by making the circle of love as big as possible. In fact, my denomination openly speaks of our living under a faith tent big enough for everyone except those who don't believe it's big enough for everyone. In this way we do not practice a "permissive" inclusion, but one that seeks to include in every way that strengthens the whole while excluding what weakens or destroys it.

This commitment to inclusion provides Bigger Christianity with a place to stand in affirming the validity of other faiths. This goes beyond mere tolerance to a genuine embracing of people from diverse religious traditions. There is unambiguous support for this attitude in both Hebrew and Christian Scriptures, none more so than the story of Jesus returning to his hometown synagogue to preach (Luke 4:16–30). After reading the messianic "Spirit of the Lord is upon me" section from Isaiah 61, Jesus declared that this passage had been fulfilled in their very hearing. Traditional interpretations suggest Jesus was talking about himself, even though he does not say so directly. The people in the synagogue must have made the same connection because their reaction was to find what he implied incredible. "Isn't this Joseph's son?" they asked. Jesus' response did not cause them to praise God for the Scripture's fulfillment. Within minutes they were enraged to the point of trying to kill him. His words must have struck them as blasphemous—not the words about himself per se, but the implication of his illustrations about the prophets Elijah and Elisha that underscored God's goodness toward non-Israelites (a widow from the Phoenician city of Sidon and a Syrian military leader). These were not words they expected to hear from the Messiah.

Some Christians today do not want to hear these words. But *big* Christians not only hear them, but want to explore their full implication for the diverse religious world we live in today. It seems reasonable to think that Jesus' openness to God's grace reaching beyond the confines of Judaism applies to Christianity. Indeed, Big Christians wonder how Christians can dare to be possessive of divine love and mercy, given texts such as this one. Monitoring who stands outside the covenant of God is a misguided task; the real challenge is to spread the message God speaks within and outside Christianity, that idolatry is the ruin of humanity and faithfulness is its salvation.

Diversity vs. Discrimination

Former president Jimmy Carter can rightly be called a "big" Christian. Since leaving office, his example of building Habitat for Humanity homes, serving as a mediator for international disputes, and writing books that reflect authentic faith has inspired the nation and the world. There are many reasons this great, humble man of peace and reconciliation is who he is. One of them surely is that despite having been reared in the racial prejudice of the Old South, he learned at his mother's knee the difference between diversity and discrimination.

The juxtaposition of these two words might strike you as odd, but there is a good reason. The opposite of diversity is not uniformity. It is discrimination. Ironically, diversity and discrimination are actually quite similar. Diversity highlights differences as a means of expanding a group to achieve variety. Discrimination, on the other hand, makes distinctions, not to highlight differences, but to eliminate them. Discrimination sees differences as negative. Diversity sees them as positive. The goal of discrimination is exclusion, whereas diversity seeks to include. Diversity affirms differences because they contribute to the health of the whole, while discrimination makes one thing the whole. Diversity does not need uniformity. Discrimination does.

The adage "birds of a feather stick together" points to a reality of human behavior that Bigger Christianity believes works against community. We are not naturally drawn to things or people different from us. Opposites may attract as individuals, but it seldom happens in group experiences. Usually we have to work at being with people different from ourselves. Because of our natural reluctance to be with people unlike ourselves, we are likely to let fear dominate our emotions and determine our attitude and actions. That fear makes us vulnerable to discrimination. This is where we are as a nation. Rather than this being "morning in America," as Ronald Reagan proclaimed, we have stepped back into yesterday, and discrimination is touted as a good thing to protect us against our fears.

My mind goes back to the lament of my friend who wants to go to church with his family, which includes a lesbian couple and a biracial couple. How long a wait is enough when it comes to discrimination? The church has discriminated against people since the beginning because of dogma and doctrine. Some of this has changed through the centuries, but we still lack the will to admit Christianity has seldom practiced what it preached, precisely because of intractable dogma and doctrine. The church has justified discrimination on the basis of moral imperatives.

Diversity offers a bigger way to live. Having Charlotte Hanni-Leach in our congregation has shown us how true this is. One Sunday in August this middle-aged woman from Cape Town, South Africa, walked into our building and sat down in the sanctuary. She had arrived in the States two months before to meet a man with whom she had been corresponding via the Internet. An active Christian in her native land, she had missed Sunday worship, so she decided to see if the members of the little church near her would let her worship with them. Our people welcomed her as if she were already one of us. She has been attending since that August morning. She and Danny, the man she came to this country to meet in person, were married in our sanctuary three months later, with the church acting as her family in preparing and hosting the wedding and reception. We even managed to set up a simulcast of the wedding, making it possible for her grown children in South Africa to see her take her vows. She has been a gift to our church family, enlarging our circle and making the rainbow colors a little brighter.

Bigger Christianity believes diversity *is* a gift from God, and that experiencing it is indicative of the way all of life should be. Discrimination makes life too small, because it ultimately makes God too small. God made women as well as men. God made homosexual people as well as heterosexual people. To justify discrimination against either women or homosexual persons being in the church or in ministry, on the basis of Scripture or church tradition, is essentially a rejection of what God has created. That is why the argument against women or homosexual persons being ordained is discriminatory. Neither can change who they are, so rejecting them as legitimate servants of God means rejecting God as creator. The argument that homosexuality is a choice is beginning to be as irrational as the fundamentalist claim that evolution is "just a theory." Bigger Christianity says that discrimination by any other name is still discrimination. Using an ancient biblical text (Leviticus 18:22; 20:13) with prescientific understanding of genetics to justify it makes it worse.

My wife, Joy, and I have a close friend who recently "came out" to us. She is a divorced mother who has suffered from depression during most of the twenty-five years we have been friends. Through the help of an experienced therapist she finally admitted to herself she was lesbian, something she had spent a lifetime suppressing. It is ludicrous to suggest she is simply making a choice. It takes a very small Christianity to say it doesn't matter, that she is morally obligated to deny her God-given instincts and remain celibate.

Bigger Christianity believes the words of the apostle Paul, "There is no longer Jew or Greek, there is no longer slave or free, there is no longer male and female; for all of you are one in Christ Jesus. And if you belong to Christ, then you are Abraham's offspring, heirs according to the promise" (Galatians 3:28–29). Liberal Christians believe these words serve as a theological basis for the inclusion of homosexual persons in the full life of the church. Oneness in Christ excludes no one who follows him.

Bigger Christianity puts people before biblical literalism or church dogma. At no point in history have fear, hatred, and war been the result of drawing the circle of God's love and grace too wide. On the other hand, fear, hatred, and war have been spawned by the circle being too small. Discrimination is an inevitable byproduct of the absence of diversity. People always fear differences they do not understand, which leads to prejudice, which in turn leads to discrimination. Diversity personalizes issues. Differences become incarnated and can no longer be abstractly debated. It is one thing to believe homosexuality is an abomination unto God. It is something quite different to look at a person you have come to know, appreciate, even love, and speak the same way. Education will not eradicate discrimination. Diversity will. That is why Bigger Christianity embraces and promotes diversity as part of the journey with Jesus.

Respectful vs. Literal

In an early morning exercise class Joy and I met two sisters we came to like very much. Soon after becoming better acquainted, they discovered I had written *What's Wrong with the Christian Right* and wanted to read it. Later they asked us to go out for coffee to discuss it. They shared their concern that I claimed that everyone interprets Scripture and that it is impossible for anyone not to interpret it. Finally I asked them if they accepted all biblical passages as literally true, such as Genesis 6:1–4:

> When people began to multiply on the face of the ground, and daughters were born to them, the sons of God saw that they were fair; and they took wives for themselves of all that they chose. Then the LORD said, "My spirit shall not abide in mortals forever, for they are flesh; their days shall be one hundred twenty years." The Nephilim were on the earth in those days—and also afterward—when the sons of God went in to the daughters of humans, who bore children to them. These were the heroes that were of old, warriors of renown.

My point in asking them about this report of heavenly beings cavorting with the daughters of humans who then bore their children was not to trick or confuse them. I simply wanted them to see that reading texts such as this one literally would always back them in a corner. Unfortunately both sisters admitted they didn't know the Bible all that well, but still believed the Bible was the word of God and that all Christians should accept it as it is. They went on to say they couldn't go to a church that didn't teach people this view of the Bible.

Obviously our effort to engage them on questions about the implications of what they were saying came to naught. Joy and I were saddened by what we heard. These intelligent, personable women have a faith made very small by a biblical literalism they cannot defend but do not want to question.

Bigger Christianity offers a different approach. Part of an introductory statement for a new twelve-week study for big Christians who take the Bible seriously but reject the doctrine of literalism reads:

> People know that at its core, Christianity has something good to offer the human race. At the same time, many have a sense that they are alone in being a thinking Christian and that "salvaging" Christianity is a hopeless task. What is needed is a safe environment where people have permission to ask the questions they have always wanted to ask but have been afraid to for fear of being thought a heretic.

This study is appropriately entitled *Living the Questions,*[13] an affirmation that faith questions are consistent with a desire to grow into spiritual maturity. Literalism fears questions, because it is a doctrine that protects already established beliefs from historical scrutiny or modern challenge. Sadly, more than a few Christians who are not literalists have thrown the baby out with the bath water, not only rejecting literalism, but giving up on the Bible itself. *Living the Questions* is a welcomed, albeit too-long-in-coming, alternative to literalism that has promise in helping Christians find the biblical grounding for Bigger Christianity. Big faith has no fear of approaching the Bible and allowing honest seekers to pursue truth wherever it may lead them.

At issue in the battle over the Bible has always been authority. Literalists believe the way to preserve biblical authority is not to question it. But Bigger Christianity says the opposite is true. Authority is preserved by the freedom interpreters have in questioning it. To understand how this is the case, let me cite an example from the way civil authority in this nation works. This is based on the experiences of Judge Harold J. Rothwax, a New York State Supreme Court justice and regular lecturer at the Columbia University law school. Judge Rothwax has the reputation of being a "tough" judge. In fact, some lawyers have labeled him "the Prince of Darkness." The title of a book he wrote, *Guilty: The Collapse of the Criminal Justice System*,[14] tells you what he thinks about what has happened to law and order in this country. Yet he describes himself as a man who has always been driven by idealism and a passion against oppression and injustice. He attributes his dual commitment to toughness and justice to a childhood in which he reacted to the firm grip of his mother "in the predictable manner of young people. I challenged her authority, just to see if I could, to establish my own style and independence."[15] What he learned at home he has carried with him throughout his legal career.

> But even though my mother was controlling, my family was loving. So while I fought against authority, I didn't hate it. I learned early on that authority can be benevolent. You could respect it and still question it. This understanding evolved into a passion for the law, and particularly for being a defense attorney. As an attorney, it was my mandate to fight against authority when it was overbearing, abusive, or unjust, but also to respect and believe in the system. When I challenged the system it was not from disrespect; rather, it was the ultimate form of respect.
>
> I understood then, as I do today, that absent challenge, authority becomes totalitarian. Authority needs to be challenged if we are to ensure the integrity of the process. It is one of the great truths of our system.[16]

Bigger Christianity views biblical authority as needing the same kind of challenge by those who respect it. Literalists, on the other hand, object by claiming God's laws are always just, are never abusive, and should not be questioned. But they don't stop here. They are also literal in how they say biblical law should be applied to contemporary life, creating a double literalism. If God's law is unchanging, circumstances are not. How law applies to these changing conditions and unexpected elements in what would otherwise be a straightforward decision requires interpretation that cannot be established in advance. What Judge Rothwax says about civil law is equally true for biblical law: "The law cries out to us to challenge every detail, to avoid rigidity, to question every firm notion, attitude, and belief. It demands that we be skeptical of the very principles we hold most dear, even as we strive to fulfill them. We are meant to squirm when issues of life and death are at stake."[17] He goes on to say, therefore, that "it is impossible for the [Supreme] Court to establish clear rules that would govern *all* future case because clear rules would have *unclear* boundaries. Applying a clear rule to an unforeseen situation can sometimes lead to unjust results."[18]

The foundation for this understanding of law and its authority is the desire always to seek truth. Literalists argue that questions undermine truth, when the opposite is the case. Truth, says Judge Rothwax, must be the primary goal of criminal procedure.[19] Bigger Christianity believes the same principle applies to the study of the Bible. The primary goal is truth. Getting to it is the hard part. To say the Bible is God's truth is not the same thing as knowing what that truth is. This is the flaw of literalism. Our approach is to have respect enough for biblical law to question and dig and challenge, using all the tools available to scholarly pursuit, in the quest to know the truth that sets people free.

From a liberal perspective, fundamentalism obscures the biblical message it seems determined to protect. No book has suffered this fate more than the last book in the Bible, The Revelation to John. Literalism has all but destroyed the good news of Revelation, as Barbara Rossing documents in her book *The Rapture Exposed.*[20] Revelation contains a message of hope that "God does not come to take us away from this earth, but rather comes to dwell with us in every joy and every sorrow, in every blazing display of nature's beauty that is never spent."[21] It was written, she points out, to encourage Christians to stay faithful and not lose heart or faith as they watch earthly powers kill and destroy. The theme in Revelation, she says, is that Jesus Christ was and is the victory of God over evil and death, a victory whose full manifestation is not only in the future, but is the future that has already begun.

Calling "the Rapture" a "racket," Rossing methodically disassembles the dispensationalist view of Revelation popularized by the Left Behind series of books by fundamentalist authors Tim LaHaye and Jerry Jenkins. Rossing goes into detail to show that not only do the authors get it wrong; they actually distort and corrupt the message John intended his readers to receive. Essentially, she says, they "fictionalize Revelation," not by using the genre of the novel to tell their stories, but precisely because they literalize Revelation's message. Thus, Rossing is unwilling to let fundamentalists off the hook for a worldview that not only anticipates, but looks forward to a Middle East Armageddon that will usher in the end of time.

> The dispensationalist version of the biblical storyline requires tribulation and war in the Middle East, not peace plans. That is the most terrifying aspect of this distorted theology. Such blessing of violence is the very reason why we cannot afford to give in to the dispensationalist version of the biblical storyline—because real people's lives are at stake.[22]

Bigger Christianity doesn't simply read the Bible in a different way than fundamentalism does. That would make the difference a matter of one view over another. The issue is much deeper and more profound. Bigger Christianity says literalism is a distortion of Scripture, a doctrine imposed on Scripture that obscures truth rather than revealing it. As Rossing writes of her work:

> As I have argued . . . the Rapture and the dispensationalist chronology is a fabrication. The dispensationalist story creates a comprehensive narrative that appeals to people who are seeking clear-cut answers. But the dispensationalist system's supposed clear-cut answers rely on a highly selective biblical literalism, as well as insertion of nonexistent two-thousand year gaps and dubious redefinitions of key terms. The system is not true to a literal reading of the Bible, as they claim. Nor is their system true to the Bible's wonderful richness and complexity. The dispensationalist system narrows the Bible's message.[23]

The Bible's richness and complexity nurtures Bigger Christianity. Literalism is not simply a different approach to the Bible; it prevents an honest reading of it. Literalism is transparent in its need to protect the authority of one interpretation over another. Bigger Christianity has no interest in this power game. Its goal is to hear a word from God that helps people of faith to live without falling into idolatry. The word "sacred writings" is a term various people of faith use when referring to the texts of their particular tradition. While this practice is understandable, it leads away from rather than toward the intended goal. The point of reading the Bible is not to be able to say the Bible is sacred. It is to make *our lives* sacred. The meaning of the word comes from the Latin *sacer,* which means "dedicated" and "holy." The goal of reading the Bible is to find help in dedicating ourselves more to God, in making our lives a holy offering to God. This is why the apostle Paul urged the Roman Christians to offer themselves as a living sacrifice, holy and acceptable to God (Romans 12:1).

Literalism turns this around and makes the Bible the object of devotion. The Bible becomes sacred and holy, rather than one's life. It lets Christians off the hook, which may explain why so many Bible-believing Christians are quick to argue about the Bible but have little to say about justice and peace and loving your enemies. Liberal Christians have no less trouble making our lives sacred offerings to God, but we at least know where the focus needs to be. We want to read and study the Bible with all our might, in the expectation that as we do, we will grow in our will and capacity to love God with equal commitment.

Common Sense vs. Legalism

Literalism inevitably leads to legalism, which is a rigid adherence to law put into practice. But the result is the opposite of the intended goal. Again, the insights of Judge Rothwax are especially helpful. He cites legalistic interpretations of what is called the "exclusionary rule" as examples of why rigid applications of law don't work. In 1977 the Supreme Court ruled that the

Fourth Amendment guarantees all citizens protection against unwarranted search and seizure. What followed was the "exclusionary rule," which means any evidence found during a search without a court-ordered warrant can be excluded from trial by the judge. But Judge Rothwax believes that in the aftermath of the Supreme Court ruling, lower courts have disregarded common sense to the point where no one understands how to apply the law. He staunchly supports protections against unfair searches, but he argues that restricting the police in using common sense in searching and seizing evidence is undermining real justice. The problem, he says, is that the exclusionary rule is *mandatory* rather than *discretionary*: "The latter uses *reasonableness* as a guide, and proposes that we try not to set detailed guidelines for police behavior in every possible situation. In its place the court will determine whether the search and seizure is reasonable by considering all relevant factors on a case-by-case basis."[24] He then sets forth several common-sense questions to determine the "reasonableness" of the search.

The broader implication of Judge Rothwax's concerns about the exclusionary rule is that whenever laws are applied to real-life situations, common sense serves the interest of laws far more than legalism. Justice can never be served when, as Supreme Court Justice Harry Blackmun observed, "We tend occasionally to strain credulity and to spin the thread of argument so thin that we depart from . . . common sense."[25] But this is precisely the effect of biblical literalism. When we declare God's laws timeless, with no flexibility in regard to contemporary circumstances, common sense is the casualty, and with it justice and mercy. But this is not the way of Bigger Christianity, which believes that common sense is essential for fairness and justice to be properly balanced.

Bigger Christianity believes that the cause of Christ is set back every time Christians choose legalism over common sense. Reverence for life cannot be enhanced when people of faith have to choose between rigidity and reality. Bigger Christianity argues that this is not a necessary choice. In fact, it says that legalism is the choice of a small faith that is resistant to making tough moral and ethical choices. The will to think eliminates legalism as an option, leaving knowledge and common sense as guides to making decisions about how to live faithfully and responsibly. Bigger Christianity believes legalism is why literalism is a dead end that forces you to come back to where you started with nothing to show for it. Morality cannot be dictated by unbending laws. The desire to distinguish between right and wrong is not nurtured and strengthened by an unreasonableness that ignores anything that might require interpreting how laws are applied to real-life circumstances.

Once Jesus entered a synagogue on the Sabbath and encountered a man with a withered hand. The legalists watched to see if he would dare violate the

laws governing the Sabbath by healing the man. The healing itself was inconsequential in comparison to their concern for legalistic adherence to the law.
In his typical wisdom, Jesus put a question to them, "Is it lawful to do good
or to do harm on the sabbath, to save life or to kill?" Our text says the crowd
was silent. Further, it says Jesus "looked around at them with anger; he was
grieved at their hardness of heart." He then healed the man's withered hand
(Mark 3:1–6).

It is not clear whether their "hardness of heart" refers to a failure to see the
real need or to their coldness in being more concerned with a commandment
than compassion. What is unmistakable, however, is that legalism is always
silent in the face of common sense. It is popular to harangue liberal Christians
for contributing to moral decline because of our willingness to be flexible in
living by biblical commands. But the real difference between bigger faith and
small faith is not that one cares about morality and the other doesn't. Rather,
it's the fact that liberals are willing to admit to the need for common sense when
deciding how to live by divine commandments. We believe, as apparently Jesus
did, that commandments are better served and preserved for the future because
of this common-sense approach. Legalism undermines the very law it pre-
sumes to follow. Liberal faith is a bigger—and better—way to live.

Sensible vs. Sectarian

"Sectarian" is often used to describe violence, because sectarianism necessarily involves a narrow outlook that divides individuals and groups. Members
of a sect share common beliefs and practices that separate and cut them off
from the larger group. "Sensible," on the other hand, means being consistent
with common sense and reason.[26]

Christian fundamentalism is an expression of sectarianism. Its beliefs,
practices, and attitudes create division within the body of Christ. The general
perception that fundamentalism differs from liberal Christianity only in what
it believes misses the significance of its sectarianism. Not all religious groups
are sectarian. Fundamentalism is, because it has no qualms about separating
itself from others, in order to avoid their corrupting influence. There is biblical precedent for this kind of attitude. When the Hebrew remnant returned
from Babylonian captivity in the fifth century before Christ, Ezra the priest
was convinced the people would survive as a people only if they separated
themselves, cut themselves off from all foreign influence. The particular focus
of concern was the non-Israelite women—"the people of the land"—the men
of Israel had taken for wives. Ezra interpreted these actions as a sign of Israel's

unfaithfulness to God because "the holy seed" had been "mixed" with the peo-
ples of the land (Ezra 9:2). Shecaniah, son of the Levite Jehiel, suggested to
Ezra that the Israelite men divorce all the foreign wives. Ezra agreed and
issued a decree to that effect:

> "You have trespassed and married foreign women, and so increased the guilt
> of Israel. Now make confession to the LORD the God of your ancestors, and
> do his will; separate yourselves from the peoples of the land and from the
> foreign wives." Then all the assembly answered with a loud voice, "It is so;
> we must do as you have said." (Ezra 10:10)

An orderly way was developed to carry out Ezra's degree. The action might
be understood as necessary in order to save the nation from idolatry. That said,
the incident is still an example of a religious sectarianism liberal Christians
find unacceptable. What is more, it didn't work. Idolatry takes many forms.
By the time of Jesus, what mattered most—the weightier matters such as justice, mercy, and faith (Matthew 23:23)—had been supplanted by a narrow
legalism. Essentially, ritualistic worship without concern for acts of justice
had become the standard.

Sectarian Christianity has never been an effective witness, even if it has
served the sectarian needs of the group. The 2004 M. Night Shyamalan film
The Village tells a story that could be about sectarianism. It is about a quiet,
isolated 1890s Pennsylvania village whose adult members supposedly made
a pact with "the creatures" residing in the surrounding woods. The towns-
people would not enter the woods, and "the creatures" would not enter the
village. From time to time, animal carcasses, devoid of fur, appear around
the village as a reminder from "the creatures" to the villagers not to break
the pact.

The village seems almost idyllic as the story unfolds, however, it quickly
becomes apparent that the close-knit community is living in constant fear of
"the creatures" in the woods. But this does not stop the curious and headstrong
Lucius Hunt from wanting to step beyond the boundaries of the town and into
the unknown. Then the predictably unexpected happens. Noah, the town's
mentally handicapped young man, who loves Ivy Walker, who loves Lucius,
attacks Lucius and leaves him for dead. Determined to get medical supplies
for him, Ivy requests permission from the village elders to go into the woods.
They consent; she goes, and returns safely, but in the process the truth is
exposed: there are no "creatures" in the woods.

The myth was told by the elders to protect the children from the world they
had left and determined never again to inhabit. In its place, they had created
the world as they wanted it to be. The film reaches its climax as the elders face

a decision: with the myth discovered, should they abandon it or continue to tell it? What the film does not address is the fact that the decision is irrelevant. The falsehood of the myth will be discovered again by the children whom it is intended to protect. Sectarianism seems a pristine way to live, but in fact it exists by illusion that is constantly under threat of exposure.

The film was based on the sectarianism of the Amish and failed to include the fact that even the Amish allow young adults to leave the community for the outside world in order to decide for themselves if Amish life is for them. But this practice is itself an acknowledgment of the futility of complete isolationism even within sectarian communities. Were the Amish to counter that it reflects their way of life needs to be a matter of choice, that would not change the fact that sectarianism is a de facto statement that a people's faith is not strong enough to survive in the real world. It fails to understand that most people want and need a faith that is sensible, realistic, and able to help them cope with the challenges of everyday life. Fundamentalism, for all its boldness in becoming a political force in today's America, seeks to persuade Christians to believe their faith is not strong enough to survive in the secular world where liberals dominate. It is as if they believe truth is an enemy of faith.

The concept of "followship" argues for a bigger faith that believes living in fear of the world's influence is not a helpful way to confront the idolatry of our age, any more than divorcing foreign wives was at the time of Ezra. Children of faith don't need to be protected from the world. They need to be equipped to live in it without being consumed by it. Cutting them off from outside influences keeps them children. Liberal Christians want their children to grow up and be able to think for themselves, so they can recognize materialistic, hedonistic seduction for what it is. Admittedly, though, we have not always been effective in empowering them to be so discerning. Indeed, we have allowed ourselves to be seduced by the dominant culture's empty claims, as we tried to teach our children not to be. The hope is that they can learn by our experience.

At the same time, this failure on our part would appear to support the case for separating from the world. But the fact is, there is no evidence that fundamentalist Christians are more effective than liberal ones in resisting worldly temptations and falling prey to human frailties. Evangelical scholar Ronald J. Sider has reminded "born again" Christians, that is, "evangelicals," that they have no better record in regard to divorce, premarital sex, domestic violence, and use of pornography than anyone else.[27] This is not a case against sectarianism per se. Evangelicals do not see themselves as trying to cut themselves off from the world. They just don't want to be shaped by it. But this is not the case with fundamentalism. Its "us vs. them" attitude is sectarianism to the core, yet it also has no better "moral" record than the rest of us.

Sensible faith means being realistic about the dangers the dominant culture poses to the values and priorities of people of faith, while also being able to challenge those dangers. Unfortunately, it seems fundamentalism's influence is having the opposite effect. Funding programs that fight AIDS here and abroad is a graphic example. Political leaders pandering to fundamentalist voters have rejected funding AIDS education groups that also distribute condoms and provide needle exchanges for drug addicts. The New Jersey State Senate, for example, in 2004 failed to pass a needle exchange bill that was approved by the State Assembly because of moral objections. Without access to clean needles or to treatment programs, which are now overcrowded, addicts risk almost certain infection by continuing to share needles with other addicts. They then spread AIDS through sexual contact to their spouses, lovers, and unborn children, endangering an ever-widening circle of lives.

Opponents argue that furnishing addicts with clean needles "legitimizes" drug use, another opinion viewed as fact that flies in the face of the evidence. Studies carried out across the United States and around the world have shown that needle exchanges slow the spread of disease without creating new intravenous-drug addicts. New Jersey has one of the highest infection rates in the country, especially in Atlantic City, the epicenter of the state's AIDS epidemic, but apparently this fact has not had an impact on those state senators being guided by ideology rather than reason.

This is microsectarianism at work in government decisions. When the influence of moralism is stronger than common-sense solutions in confronting a worldwide problem like AIDS or hunger, the effect is sectarianism in miniature. Cutting yourself off from the real world, either as a community or by way of particular decisions, produces similar results. Christianity is seen by others as a faith ill equipped to deal with the real problems in the real world.

Bigger Christianity believes that a sensible faith is a better witness. Rather than compromising the Christian message, it is a way to make its influence stronger. Escaping the world is an internal task that empowers Christians to be big enough to be in the world but not of it.

Science as Friend vs. Science as Foe

Another consequence of biblical literalism is an ongoing battle between science and religion—a battle that not only makes no sense to Bigger Christianity, but does not have to be fought. Science does not create facts. It uncovers them through a process of trial and error. Science didn't make the earth a planet. It discovered it was. So, too, with the rotation of the earth around the

sun, gravity, black holes, and thousands of other amazing discoveries. Einstein described science as "the century-old endeavor to bring together by
means of systematic thought the perceptible phenomena of this world into as
thorough-going association as possible."[28] To pit faith against such uncovering is both unnecessary and foolish. Each time the Bible has fought against
science, it has lost, and always will. The fact that the Catholic Church finally
admitted its error in condemning Galileo (and Copernicus) for the outrageous
discovery that the earth revolved around the sun—rather than vice versa, as
the church had insisted—is a testament to the futility of faith feuding with science. The deck is stacked against us.

The irony of the church's condemnation of Galileo was that he was actually
a man of faith who did not believe he was undermining faith or the church's
authority. Bigger Christianity stands in the Galilean tradition. It does not
believe science is an enemy of Scripture. Rather, it affirms science as an expression of reason, which historically has been a key element in our ability to serve
God. "Heart" in Israel's Shema—"Hear, O Israel: The LORD is our God, the
LORD alone. You shall love the LORD your God with all your heart, and with all
your soul, and with all your might" (Deuteronomy 6:4–5)—means "mind."
When Jesus repeated this call to devotion, he told his disciples to love God with
heart and mind (Matthew 22:37), as if to underscore the fact that love is an act
of the will. Sadly, Christian fundamentalism has created a modern conflict
between faith and reason, heart and mind. This has contributed to people like
the two sisters mentioned earlier who are not allowing facts to get in the way
of their opinions. In small Christianity all facts are opinions and all opinions
are facts. Thus, fundamentalists feel justified in believing the world is about
ten thousand years old, despite established facts to the contrary. Evolution is
just a theory, one opinion in a world where facts don't exist.

The best scientists acknowledge the subjective element in discovery. The
observer inevitably influences what is observed, even as the observed is independent of the observer. In general we see what we want to see, but what we
see is not all there is. Absolute human knowledge, then, is to a degree subjective and always open to correction. But none of this leads to the conclusion
that science doesn't know anything, or that there is no scientific knowledge.
Since the seventeenth-century Enlightenment we have come to realize that
truth is not limited to scientific experimentation. In addition, we now see that
right and wrong do have a role in how science is used, even in determining if
there are limits to legitimate scientific experiment. In other words, science and
ethics belong in the same room, despite being distinct fields of inquiry.

This balance between ethics and science is not helped by fundamentalist
Christians speaking as if they alone care about it. To oppose stem-cell research,

as if those who support it are showing a wanton disregard for all forms of life, is itself morally suspect. The issue is not whether moral judgments have a role in scientific decisions. The capacity to build space weapons, for example, does not justify doing so. In the words of Einstein, "knowledge of what *is* does not open the door directly to what *should be*."[29] The real issue is the degree of wisdom one shows in weighing how morality and science work together. Not only did Einstein reject the notion that religion and science were in an "unreconcilable conflict"; he believed that when the role of both was properly understood, such a conflict was impossible.[30] He summed up his view this way: "Science without religion is lame; religion without science is blind."[31]

That is the position of Bigger Christianity as well. My father taught my brothers and me never to start a needless fight or one we couldn't win. That is precisely what fundamentalism has done with science. For the sake of its children, who cannot live outside the world of science, Christianity can be bigger than this and, thereby, also better. Learning again from the wisdom of the great Einstein, "the further the spiritual evolution of [humankind] advances, the more certain it seems to me that the path to genuine religiosity does not lie through the fear of life, and the fear of death, and blind faith, but through the striving after rational knowledge."[32]

Curiosity vs. Anti-intellectualism

Underlying fundamentalism's fight with science is a pervading anti-intellectualism. This statement is not just a liberal bias, according to evangelical scholar Mark Noll. In his provocative book *The Scandal of the Evangelical Mind*,[33] he states that for Christians "the life of the mind" is "to think like a Christian—to think within a specifically Christian framework—across the whole spectrum of modern learning."[34] This spectrum includes science, economics, literary criticism, philosophy, history, and so forth. We have already suggested that being Christian has to do with how one sees the world as a follower of Jesus Christ. Noll's "evangelical mind," then, would "see" the world through the eyes of being an evangelical Christian.

But what is an evangelical? Noll essentially agrees with British historian David Bebbington, who identified the following elements of evangelicalism: (1) conversion, or an emphasis on "new birth," that is, being "born again"; (2) biblicism, or reliance on the Bible as the ultimate religious authority; (3) crucicentrism, or the centrality of the redeeming work of Christ on the cross.[35] While evangelicalism has never been a cohesive movement, Noll believes these are the key ingredients of an evangelical faith. What is absent from the list—and is of most concern for our purposes—is biblical literalism, which lies at the core of fundamentalism. Indeed, it is precisely this literalism that has propelled evangelicalism into the "scandal" Noll addresses. He laments the fact that evangelicalism has drifted from once-invigorating intellectual inquiry into an anti-intellectualism that believes learning is not only unnecessary for the development of faith, but counterproductive.[36]

In particular, Noll pulls no punches in criticizing dispensational premillennialism, which focuses exclusively on scenarios of how modern events are leading to the imminent end of the world. The consequence, Noll argues, is that evangelicalism has ceased to be a force to be reckoned with in the intellectual arena, where secular thinking now dominates. Instead, it lives primarily within its own circle of the like-minded, without any significant influence in the halls of colleges and universities where Freud and Darwin are encountered daily. Fundamentalism, along with Pentecostalism, was a response to the new nineteenth-century biblical scholarship, constituting what Noll calls "a disaster for the life of the mind" among evangelicals. In short, fundamentalism has been the primary cause of evangelicalism's losing the battle for the modern mind. While polls consistently show that the majority of Christians who attend church on any given Sunday identify themselves with evangelicalism, Noll says that, with few exceptions, evangelicalism as an intellectual discipline has no currency in the major universities in America and Europe.

Noll confirms what Bigger Christianity has known for a long time. At bottom, biblical literalism is an expression of anti-intellectualism that has produced a host of antiscientific claims—that the world is ten thousand years old, that the Genesis stories of creation and Adam and Eve are historical, that an imminent "rapture" will carry the faithful to heaven, that Israel must control the whole of Jerusalem and rebuild the ancient temple to prepare the way for the return of Christ. Noll himself points out that in general this anti-intellectualism leads to one of two responses to the complexities of the modern world and the secular wisdom that gives its direction. One is to withdraw, or to remain silent in the face of "real-life complexities of the present age."[37] The other is to mount a public crusade. This, he says, has been the way of the Christian Right, who "filled with righteous anger" have attempted to "recoup . . . public losses through political confrontation."[38]

Noll is not a liberal Christian, but his kind of evangelicalism certainly admits to the reality of biblical interpretation that fundamentalism denies, as well as sharing Bigger Christianity's concern about fundamentalism's impact on the public image of Christianity. Scientific knowledge is not the enemy of Christianity. As we have already pointed out, Christians may rightly challenge the claims of scientific objectivism, but that is different from trying to turn religious claims into "science." To affirm that there are different ways of "knowing," as Christians do, should not be interpreted to mean pitting knowledge as science or history against faith. Going beyond the rational does not require one to become anti-intellectual.

Confessional vs. Dogmatic

We are now ready to state the obvious: Bigger Christianity is confessional rather than dogmatic. Bigger Christianity witnesses and testifies to what it sees, rather than insisting that it knows all the truth. It admits to and makes known what it believes, thinks, and wants to do. Confessing is an act of disclosure. Dogma, on the other hand, is a system of doctrines to be accepted without scrutiny or critique. They are true because the church says they are. It is not surprising, therefore, that to be dogmatic means to express beliefs "in an authoritative, often arrogant way."[39] Sadly, arrogance seems to be an unavoidable consequence of dogma. That the church is dogmatic strikes me as one of the great contradictions of life. Nothing in the Gospels suggests Jesus was dogmatic. He was more concerned with right actions than right beliefs. That is why Bigger Christianity asserts that confessing is more consistent with the way of Jesus than dogmatism. To be confessional eliminates the temptation to be arrogant.

Dogmatism depends on the bogus argument that the church has to speak with authority on matters of faith and morals, to avoid heresy and debauchery. If history is a guide, dogmatism has failed on both counts. Concern with heresy, which is mostly in the eye of the beholder, involves church teaching, but not righteous behavior. Heresy says that what you believe or don't believe can exclude you from the church, even if you live a righteous life. Thus, dogmatism leads Christians onto the slippery slope of being more concerned about being right than about being Christlike.

Being confessional does not ignore the need for the church to identify core beliefs and values. It simply wants to couch them in ways that allow for discussion, dissent, and revision. Our congregation has identified the core beliefs that give us identity and core values that give us direction. But we have done so without forcing compliance for those who would have us say something else or nothing at all. Being confessional sets outer boundaries instead of drawing an inner circle in which everyone must stand to be in full communion. Confession affirms the importance of belief without making it narrow or tyrannical.

One of the major weaknesses of dogmatism is that it depends on the church's ignoring its own fallibility. The Protestant Reformation was a revolt against the corruption of the Roman Catholic Church, but Protestants soon began to repeat the mistake. Today Protestant fundamentalists are no less dogmatic than the Catholic Church. They are also alike in being unwilling to admit that they hide their weaknesses in order to protect their position of power.

Dogmatism will never disappear, but neither will it ever finally win the day. Consider the fact that the widespread use of contraceptives and a high divorce rate are facts of life in Italy, arguably the most Catholic country in the world. Confession, on the other hand, has an enduring appeal without a need for external authority. It thrives on attraction rather than power. It discloses instead of coercing. It speaks with conviction but without arrogance. Bigger Christianity is confessional because it knows stories have more power than dogma. That is what a confession is. It's the story of your journey of faith. By its nature others can relate to it without feeling compelled to walk the way you have chosen. No wonder Jesus told stories instead of giving commandments.

Confession builds community. People connect with one another at a basic level that creates a bond that transcends individualism. Dogmatism does not connect people to each other. It connects them to doctrine that is considered more important than relationships. Confession rejects this kind of depersonalization of faith. It values people above power, journey above doctrine, and persuasion above compulsion. This is why confession makes Christianity bigger and stronger than dogmatism can. People bonded together through the stories they tell and the confessions of faith they make create a community that can withstand the forces working against it much more effectively than a community held together by dogmatic propositions members may or may not actually believe.

My own denomination is an example of how Christians can be bonded together through confession rather than dogma. We do not use creeds to define our faith, nor do we insist on a single statement of faith everyone must follow to be in fellowship with us. The closest we have come to a statement of beliefs is called "The Disciples Affirmation of Faith." It is our confession of faith, not something imposed on church members or clergy. As such, it shows the power of confession to unite people around common bonds of faith. It reads as follows:

> As members of the Christian Church, we confess that Jesus is the Christ, the Son of the living God, and proclaim him Lord and Savior of the world. In Christ's name and by his grace we accept our mission of witness and service to all people. We rejoice in God, maker of heaven and earth, and in the covenant of love which binds us to God and one another. Through baptism

into Christ we enter into newness of life and are made one with the whole people of God. In the communion of the Holy Spirit we are joined together in discipleship and in obedience to Christ. At the table of the Lord we celebrate with thanksgiving the saving acts and presence of Christ. Within the universal church we receive the gift of ministry and the light of scripture. In the bonds of Christian faith we yield ourselves to God that we may serve the One whose kingdom has no end. Blessing, glory and honor be to God forever. Amen.

This Affirmation of Faith underscores that by nature confessional statements are nonjudgmental. As we have noted, once the use of creeds emerged in the fourth-century church, concern for doctrinal purity became another name for judgmentalism. Bigger Christianity believes confession is a solid foundation for an enduring Christian witness. People stay together when they are bound by faith that is consensual and open to new insights and new directions. The church has relied on dogmatism for too long. In an age where information on any subject is a mouse click away, Christianity must steer a different course. An emphasis on confessional statements of faith is an answer that is both bigger and better, and is consistent with the view that the heart of discipleship is following Jesus, rather than simply believing in him.

Justice vs. Righteousness

The Southern Baptist Convention, meeting in Nashville, Tennessee, the week of June 23, 2005, announced it was ending an eight-year boycott of the Walt Disney Company for violating "moral righteousness and traditional family values." This specific "violation" was Disney's decision to provide benefits to the partners of gay and lesbian employees.[40] The Baptists said the boycott had served its purpose, but in truth it had had no impact on Disney operations and did not force the company to abandon its benefit policies.

"Moral righteousness" is a favorite phrase for fundamentalist Christians. The judgmentalism it produces in them clearly runs counter to the admonition Jesus gave: "Why do you see the speck in your neighbor's eye, but do not notice the log in your own eye?" (Matthew 7:3). Just as noteworthy, though, is the fact it blinds them to the issues of justice their moral crusades ignore. "To do justice" is what the Lord requires of you, says the prophet Micah (6:8). Numerous parables Jesus told say the same thing, none more so than the Rich Man and Lazarus (Luke 16:19–31). Lazarus was a beggar who sat at the front gate of a rich man's home. He longed for the crumbs from the rich man's table as dogs licked his wounds, suggesting he was a leper. Both men died. Lazarus went to God. The rich man went to hell. Begging for mercy but receiving none, the rich man requested to father Abraham to send Lazarus to warn his five brothers not to follow in his footsteps. Abraham responded, "If they do not listen to Moses and the prophets, neither will they be convinced even if someone rises from the dead."

That Christians should be people of good character is obvious. That moral purity is the measure of a true Christian is not. Bifurcating morality and justice has no basis in Hebrew or Christian Scripture, but it does allow fundamentalism to oversimplify issues such as abortion and homosexuality. They say, for example, that liberal Christians believe in abortion and support candidates who support the *Roe v. Wade* landmark Supreme Court ruling. But the charge is false. Abortion is a terrible choice for anyone to make. But we believe it should not be isolated from important matters of justice that are usually present. Liberal Christians believe the choice of a rape victim to have an abortion is a justice issue as well as a moral dilemma. The same is true for a victim of incest, or when the mother's life is at risk. The birth of a child to a "child" mother is a justice issue. The pregnancy of a mother in a third-world nation who cannot feed the ten children she already has also raises a question of justice.

In a perfect world, abortion is not a choice a moral person would make. But no such world exists. Liberal Christians understand that this means morality and justice can clash at the point of human decision making. This conflict is why a choice cannot be dictated in advance to apply to all situations. As we suggested in the earlier discussion on legalism, laws and principles cannot anticipate any and all future circumstances. The freedom to make a choice is a necessary part of balancing the concern for justice with personal morality. Unfortunately, Christian fundamentalists do not believe in this need for balance. They are committed to their antiabortion position without regard to matters related to justice. Their rigidity is why liberal Christians who personally support limited choice are hesitant to promote it as a public policy. Fundamentalists are already engaged in promoting legal limits in the hope of one day eliminating choice altogether. Commitment to social justice, therefore, is why liberal Christians support the right of women to choose. "Legal, safe, and rare," as President Bill Clinton put it, is the position Bigger Christianity takes.

The judgmentalism of Christian fundamentalists on this issue has led to many problems beyond abortion itself. One is an inflexible position on federal funding for stem-cell research. To argue that using stem cells in a Petri dish kept in a refrigerator is equivalent to committing murder strikes liberal Christians as unjust. The reality is that diseases such as Parkinson's, Alzheimer's, and diabetes are already killing people. Stem-cell research holds promise for finding a cure for all of them. We need only to consider the debilitating impact of a disease like diabetes to understand the shortsightedness of this kind of moralism.

When I first met Earl, he was not quite forty years old. Other than having to inject insulin into his body three times a day, he was still able to work and occasionally to play a round of golf. Seven years later, he is virtually homebound, except for being rushed to the hospital every six weeks. The longest he has gone without hospitalization in the last three years is eleven weeks. Heart and lung problems have become chronic. He has suffered several minor strokes, and two years ago he went into a diabetic coma that lasted for six weeks. The persistent buildup of fluid in his legs has made walking all but impossible.

Earl's story is not the picture most people have of diabetes. Because many of us have known healthy-looking people testing their blood for insulin levels, we are more likely to view it as an inconvenient disease than one that is truly life threatening. But according to the American Diabetes Association, diabetes was the sixth leading cause of death listed on U.S. death certificates in 2000. On 69,301 death certificates, diabetes was listed as the underlying cause of death, and diabetes contributed to 213,062 deaths. Further, diabetes is likely to be underreported as a cause of death, because many decedents with diabetes do not have the disease entered on their death certificate. Studies have found that, among persons for whom diabetes contributed to their death, only about 35–40 percent have it listed anywhere on the certificate and only 10–15 percent have it listed as the underlying cause of death.

Small Christianity believes stem-cell research kills babies. Bigger Christianity believes it is a noble effort to prevent the suffering of people like Earl. Small Christianity claims we should not take one life for the sake of another, but in an ironic twist, that is precisely what they are choosing to do. Earl hopes he will live long enough to see his two adolescent daughters graduate from high school. He may not. Bigger Christianity wonders how it could be morally wrong to support funding for responsible research that might make his wish more possible. Small Christianity's resistance seems to us to be a case of rigid moralism standing in the way of common sense. That is why liberal Christians believe the just and right thing to do is to choose a father's life over a human cell.

Another tangential issue to abortion on which fundamentalists have begun to focus their judgmentalism is the removal of artificial life support, as we noted in chapter 1 regarding Terri Schiavo. But it was the politicization of this tragedy that was so appalling. For the first time in our history the U.S. Congress passed a law that applied to one person only. It required the federal court of Atlanta to review the case for yet another time, President Bush having rushed back from his ranch in Crawford, Texas, to sign the legislation. He justified his dramatic action by saying he felt obligated to err on the side of life. What went underreported at the time was the fact that at the same time the president was signing the Schiavo law, six-month-old Sun Hudson, who suffered from a fatal congenital disease, died after a Texas hospital removed his feeding tube. Without the resources to pay his medical costs or find another institution to take him, the hospital was permitted to take this action under the Texas Futile Care Law signed by then-governor George W. Bush. Later, when the federal court refused to stop the Schiavo feeding tube from being removed and also rebuked the Congress for politicizing the case, House majority leader Tom DeLay, who in the fall of 2005 was forced to give up his leadership post while under Texas indictment for money laundering, said judges were "out of control" and threatened them with congressional action: "The Constitution gives [Congress] the responsibility to create courts. If we can create them, we can uncreate them."[41]

If this were not enough, Florida Governor Jeb Bush asked the state's attorney for Pinellas County to "take a fresh look" at why Terri collapsed fifteen years before, implying that her husband did something nefarious to her. At the time of the request, it was obvious that attorney Bernie McCabe had no enthusiasm for this inquiry. As he told *New York Times* columnist Bob Herbert, "The governor's asked me to do something, and I'm going to try to do it."[42] Bush's actions, as Herbert pointed out, were the height of the abuse of political power, as became clear when only a few weeks later McCabe reported there was no basis for further review and the governor dropped the matter.

Jeb Bush's actions were at best an egregious abuse of power. There had been an initial investigation into why Terri Schiavo collapsed. No evidence existed that a crime had been committed. Yet the governor of a state, having been rebuffed by the courts and an autopsy report confirming that Terri suffered from irreparable brain damage, launched an investigation into the life of a private citizen.

But the story did not end there. Terri Schiavo's parents and siblings also continued their campaign of impugning the motives of people who supported the numerous court rulings that permitted the feeding tube to be removed. In a statement during a right-to-life convention in Minneapolis in the spring of 2005, and at the time the autopsy report was released, Terri's sister, Suzanne Vitadamo, said her family dismissed the significance of the report: "We all knew that Terri was seriously brain-injured before the report. The . . . medical examiner report also confirms that Terri was not terminal . . . that Terri had a strong heart, and that Terri was brutally dehydrated to death."[43] *Brutally dehydrated.* That is what

Michael Schiavo, the doctors and nurses, his attorney, and everyone who supported his decision did to Terri Schiavo, according to her sister.

This language is not only judgmental, but grossly uninformed about how doctors and hospitals approach end-of-life issues. Whenever a patient has an advance medical directive, or what used to be called a living will, family and physicians are legally obligated to follow a patient's previously stated wishes, except in a case where this goes against the patient's best interest. It is a good thing such discretion exists. Our doctor son often treats patients with life-threatening illnesses. He says it is common to encounter a patient or family with a medical directive that does not say what they think it says. One of his patients had a directive that included a *Do Not Intubate* request. This meant this young adult in his late 20s did not want to be put on a breathing machine. But when our son asked if that included a situation such as his developing pneumonia where he might need help breathing for a brief period, his answer was no. Under those circumstances, he said he would want to be intubated. But that was not what his directive said.

Part of the reason this happens is that the more specific the directive is, the more difficult it is to follow. Physicians generally advise that medical directives be more an expression of values and wishes than specific instructions for situations no one can anticipate. In the absence of directives, doctors and families try their best to do what they believe the patient would decide to do if they were in a position to make the decision. In all instances they err on the side of caution. Yet the right-to-life movement claims there is a pervasive "culture of death" in this country that puts all disabled and incapacitated people in jeopardy, as if "liberal" doctors (a rare breed, truth be told) and families are waiting for the opportunity to put them to death. In a recent newspaper column, a radical right-wing commentator likened this "culture of death" environment to what existed in Nazi Germany.

> Currently, the U.S. Holocaust Memorial Museum in Washington, D.C., is staging an exhibit that offers food for thought on this issue. The exhibit is called "Deadly Medicine: Creating the Master Race." It examines the idea of "lebensunwertes Leben"—lives not worthy of life—which the Nazis used to justify their elimination of thousands deemed unfit to live: the retarded, the "defective" and the seriously ill.
>
> Some German intellectuals championed this idea well before the Nazi era began. A 1920 book, for example, decried "the meticulous care shown to existences which are not just absolutely worthless"—the disabled and deformed—"but even of negative value." It called for applying the "healing remedy" of premature death, in order to "eliminat[e] those who were born unfit for life or who later became so."

Today, we must ensure that we ourselves are not tempted to start down
this slippery slope—moved by free choice rather than totalitarian edict, and
seduced by a shallow notion of "death with dignity."[44]

The possibility of respectful dialogue would be enhanced if fundamentalists would argue against liberal Christian positions without personal attacks.
Sadly, they do not appear to be able to resist this temptation. In a *Washington
Post* story, Alan Cooperman claimed there was an effort among some conservative and liberal Christians to find common ground on these hot-button social
issues. He used the Reverend Rob Schenck, a Christian Right youth leader, as
an example, quoting Schenck as saying that he planned to tell young evangelicals at an upcoming Christian music festival that he now believes homosexuality is not a choice but a "predisposition." "That may not sound shocking to
you," Schenck said, "but it will be shocking to my audience."

Though Cooperman interpreted Schenck's new perspective as proof that he
was seeking a middle ground on homosexuality, Schenck himself disagrees.
According to the Agape Press online news report, Schenck claims Cooperman
misrepresented his position: "Same-sex relationships on an erotic and sexual,
physical level are sin. They are wrong, they need to be repented of, and they
need to be remedied. Mr. Cooperman obviously had an editorial objective in
his article. He took my comments out of that context and shaped them and
used them to achieve his own goals—and frankly I resent it, because I was
very, very clear with Mr. Cooperman."[45]

The irony is that it actually does not matter whether Cooperman took
Schenck's comment about homosexual orientation out of context or not. In
response to its publication, Schenck asserted, "There is no room for compromise on the sanctity of human life, the sanctity of marriage and the public
acknowledgment of God." If these words represent a middle ground to Cooperman, it is unlikely that is how gay and lesbian persons will hear it. Nor do liberal Christians hear it that way. Although Schenck may actually believe
homosexuality is a sexual "predisposition," it obviously has no effect on how
he thinks gay and lesbian persons should live. In essence he is saying, "I now
understand why you are gay, but I don't support your living as if you are."

If you know a gay or lesbian person, you know how unjust and moralistic
this kind of attitude is. My wife and I met a gay couple several months ago
who have adopted three children. We were privileged to be invited into their
home. Tom is a university professor and Adam writes computer software programs. We saw firsthand the loving environment these two partners of twenty
years have created for these children no one else seemed to want. The children act as normal as any others their age. In fact, that is how all the relation-

ships seemed to us. The difference between this home and the others we know is that the children have two dads. But these are not just any dads. These are smart and loving men who are very aware of the full scope of the emotional needs of their children. They go out of their way to put the children in situations in which they encounter healthy female role models, not unlike single moms wanting their children to find male role models.

We came away from this experience more convinced than ever that the anti–gay marriage amendments spreading through many states are an example of Christian fundamentalists ignoring facts in order to promote abject discrimination against gays and lesbians. The reality is that the majority of all marriages in this country take place between a man and a woman who have already been living together. On more than one occasion I have performed a marriage ceremony in which children of these couples have participated. What is more, there is a trend at the moment for brides to have their wedding gown tapered to show off their pregnancy. A recent news items told this story of Neomi Padilla, 32:

> For her wedding last year before 100 guests at the historic Mission Inn in Riverside, California . . . [she] wore a sexy spaghetti-strap dress from L'ezu Atelier in Newport Beach and four-inch heels. . . . At the altar, she was unable to kneel comfortably. "My husband held me because I thought I'd fall," she said. Making her way down a staircase to the reception, things got more precarious. Being seven months pregnant, she couldn't see her feet.[46]

The Rev. Scott Carpenter, a Unity Church pastor who presides over the National Association of Wedding Ministers, said that pregnant brides account for about 20 percent of the weddings he performs.

If the "sanctity" of traditional marriage is under assault, how is it that cohabitation is less of a culprit than the union of gays and lesbians who make up 2 percent of the population? Yet there is no sign anyone is promoting an anticohabitation constitutional amendment or an antidivorce amendment. The reason is obvious enough. There is no political support for either. Bigger Christianity believes that the margins by which amendments against gay marriage are being passed are a sobering reminder that Americans have yet to learn the self-destructive impact open discrimination against one another has on our common life. A just society is one in which all citizens enjoy the same freedoms and the same restrictions, living equally under the same laws.

Liberal Christians cannot endorse laws that prevent gay and lesbian partners from enjoying the legal rights pertaining to heterosexual love relationships. It is difficult to understand why any Christian would support denying our friends Tom and Adam hospital visiting rights for one another because they do not have legal status as partners. Fundamentalist Christians insist they are not discriminating against homosexuals, but the same complaint was made by the owner of Patterson's Drug Store in my hometown of Lynchburg, Virginia, when he argued that as a business owner it was his right to refuse to serve anybody he wanted to at his all-white lunch counter. Most white churches agreed, since the gospel preached in them claimed that integration would lead to intermarriage, which in turn would lead to the ruination of the white race. This history makes the support for anti–gay marriage amendments by black clergy all the more baffling. They saw right through the racist claims of white business owners then, but they do not see the discrimination of their own attitudes today.

Liberal Christians believe Christianity should be not only bigger than this, but also smarter. The civil rights movement taught all of us that we have a stake in what is happening. Justice denied to one, Martin Luther King Jr. repeated again and again, is justice denied to all. That wisdom gives the Christian community all the more reason to be a voice of justice before this expression of homophobic frenzy succeeds in doing in every state something that a more enlightened future generation will have to undo. Our heritage is one that tells us God measures our "righteousness" by how we treat others, which is why liberal Christianity is bigger and better than the small Christianity promoting discrimination against gays and lesbians.

We mentioned earlier an article by Senator Danforth, in which he wrote, "To assert that I am on God's side and you are not, that I know God's will and you do not, and that I will use the power of government to advance my understanding of God's kingdom is certain to produce hostility." He then added, "Aware that even our most passionate ventures into politics are efforts to carry the treasure of religion in the earthen vessel of government, we proceed in a spirit of humility lacking in our conservative colleagues."

The wisdom of the senator's observations exposes the difference between a commitment to justice and passing moral judgment on others. Liberal Christians believe justice is too serious a matter to be treated with gross oversimplification and unsupportable charges. Indeed, Scripture says justice is a form of worship:

> Is not this the fast that I choose: to loose the bonds of injustice, to undo the thongs of the yoke, to let the oppressed go free, and to break every yoke? Is it not to share your bread with the hungry, and bring the homeless poor into your house; when you see the naked, to cover them, and not to hide yourself from your own kin? (Isaiah 58:6–7)

The answer to the prophet's question is, of course, "Yes." But he also declares that our own well-being is woven into the fabric of practicing justice: "Then your light shall break forth like the dawn, and your healing shall spring up quickly; your vindicator shall go before you, the glory of the LORD shall be your rear guard" (58:8).

That is the way of Bigger Christianity. In the face of complicated and morally vexing questions, it dares to try to balance justice and morality. It is not an easy task, but practicing justice never is. Often a majority will oppose a just cause. But justice is not a popularity contest. It is the will of God.

Integrity vs. Power

Power corrupts, Lord Acton observed, and absolute power corrupts absolutely. In contrast, *integrity* refers to the state of being unimpaired, having soundness. We usually think of a person of integrity as someone whose word can be trusted. That is the cornerstone of having sound judgment on which others can rely. But when power begins its corrupting ways, integrity is among its first casualties. Empirical evidence suggests that integrity and power always live in tension with one another, and when you tip toward one, you automatically move away from the other. A reach for power invariably means a test of integrity. Sometimes, when power comes to a person not seeking it, integrity can be maintained through diligence. But on the whole, the table of power offers no seat to integrity. American theologian Reinhold Niebuhr reminded a past generation of the wisdom of Henry Adams, who said that "power is poison"—so poisonous, Niebuhr said, that it "blinds the eyes of moral insight and lames the will of moral purpose."[47]

Christianity has failed to be sufficiently self-reflective about the extent to which power has been corrupting in its own household, especially when it has tried to serve as a partner to the state in establishing a "Christian" empire. That legacy continues today in the uncritical support Christian fundamentalism is giving to the Bush administration's "war on terrorism." No issue is more transparent in this regard than the prison abuse scandals at Abu Ghraib and Guantánamo Bay. There was silence from Christian fundamentalists when the Abu Ghraib prison scandal broke: no call for an investigation outside the military, no criticism of the administration's failure to deal with reports of abuse until they became public. But fundamentalists have been very vocal about the Guantánamo Bay prison camp, except that they have criticized the critics. Columnist Cal Thomas is one example. In what he called an effort to put the scandal in perspective, he attributed complete credibility to the assessment of what has happened and continues to happen at Guantánamo.

After months of complaints from reporters and interest groups about alleged mistreatment of prisoners at the Guantanamo Bay, Cuba detention facilities, the Chairman of the Joint Chiefs of Staff has set the record straight.

Appearing on Fox News Sunday, General Richard Myers denied that the terror suspects are being mistreated. . . .

Of the detainees, he said they are the kind of people, if released, who would "turn around and slit our throats (and) slit our children's throats."

The General said "this is a different kind of struggle, a different kind of war."

General Myers said the military had detained 68,000 people since the September 11, 2001 terror attacks and investigated 325 complaints of mistreatment. He said 100 cases of mistreatment have been discovered and 100 people have been punished.

That's putting it into perspective.

How many terrorist acts, including beheadings, have been punished? The answer is none.

Just to put it in perspective.[48]

That *is* one perspective, but there are others, such as a 2004 report by the FBI that included the observation: "On a couple of occasions, I entered interview rooms to find a detainee chained hand and foot in a fetal position to the floor, with no chair, food or water. Most times they had urinated or defecated on themselves and had been left there for 18, 24 hours or more."[49]

Those who have been abused have faces. One is a detainee named Mohamed al-Kahtani. He is from Saudi Arabia and is suspected of being another of the 9/11 hijackers, except that he was unable to enter the United States. According to a detailed log, al-Kahtani was interrogated for as long as twenty hours at a stretch. At one point he was put on an intravenous drip and given three and a half bags of fluid. When he asked for permission to urinate, guards told him that he first had to answer their questions. Not satisfied with his responses, the interrogator told him to urinate in his pants. He did. Thirty minutes later, according to the log, al-Kahtani was "beginning to understand the futility of his situation." In describing al-Kahtani's treatment, an FBI report said a dog was used "in an aggressive manner to intimidate" him. Again, according to the log, al-Kahtani's interrogator told him that he needed to learn, like a dog, to show respect: "Began teaching detainee lessons such as stay, come and bark to elevate his social status to that of a dog. Detainee became very agitated."[50]

The hundred cases of abuse General Myers said had been discovered, with a hundred people punished, does not include any from Guantánamo, which has been at the center of the most damaging charges of American prisoner abuse. Moreover, it is where our government is holding prisoners without any access to due process "as long as the war on terror lasts," and no one is expecting it to end any time soon.

Apparently Mr. Thomas and other Christian fundamentalists who support this kind of treatment of prisoners are not bothered by the fact that it contradicts the gospel. The best face to put on their position is that they can be Christian and support our government's unjust and inhumane treatment of prisoners, but they cannot justify their support on Christian principles. At the same time, this support does no service to our nation's reputation in the world. Perhaps no one understands this better than former president Jimmy Carter. In a statement that reflects the Bigger Christianity this book is espousing, he said, "To demonstrate clearly our nation's historic commitment to protect human rights, our government needs to close down Guantánamo and the two dozen secret detention facilities run by the United States as soon as practicable."[51] In a July 2005 speech to the Baptist World Alliance's centenary conference in Birmingham, England, Mr. Carter expanded his criticism:

> I think what's going on in Guantanamo Bay and other places is a disgrace to the U.S.A. I wouldn't say it's the cause of terrorism, but it has given impetus and excuses to potential terrorists to lash out at our country and justify their despicable acts. . . .
>
> What has happened at Guantanamo Bay . . . does not represent the will of the American people. I'm embarrassed about it, I think it's wrong.[52]

In his most recent book, *Our Endangered Values,* Mr. Carter addresses the prisoner abuse issue in detail. He recounts the story about George Washington establishing an innovative "policy of humanity" in response to a British practice during the Revolutionary War called "no quarter be granted." This meant that all captured American prisoners were summarily executed. Washington condemned the practice when he announced his policy of humanity. Using Washington's decision as a backdrop, Mr. Carter issues a challenge to all of us when he writes:

> It is an embarrassing tragedy to see a departure from our nation's historic leadership as a champion of human rights, with the abandonment defended by top officials. Only the American people can redirect our government's legal, religious, and political commitments to these ancient and unchanging moral principles.[53]

Even though Mr. Carter is a Democrat, this is not a partisan issue. Some Republican leaders share Mr. Carter's concerns. In the 2005–06 session of Congress, Senators John McCain, John Warner, and Lindsay Graham, all Republicans and members of the Senate Armed Services Committee (Warner is chairman), offered an amendment to a Pentagon appropriations bill that would prohibit cruel, inhumane, or degrading treatment of detainees in U.S. custody. While others argue that the Guantánamo prisoners are terrorists who don't deserve any canopy of protection, Senator McCain went to the core of the issue when he made an appeal on behalf of his amendment by saying the debate "is not about who they [terrorists] are. It's about who we are." He went on to say that Americans "hold ourselves" to a higher standard.[54] Former Navy admiral John Hutson, now president of the Franklin Pierce Law Center in Concord, New Hampshire, went even further in his assessment of the damage prisoner abuse is doing to our standing in the world, arguing that if the United States fails to take appropriate steps with regard to the humane treatment of detainees, we will "have changed the DNA of what it means to be an American."[55] Though the administration lobbied intensely to defeat the McCain amendment, led by Vice President Dick Cheney, the White House finally dropped its opposition when it recognized its efforts were futile.

Bigger Christianity does not believe the war on terror gives the United States permission to treat prisoners inhumanely to get information from them. It is ultimately self-defeating to think that if abusing someone who wants to "slit our throats" saves one American life, it is worth it. Moreover, abandoning Geneva Conventions will put American soldiers in foreign lands at greater risk. Both morally and practically, prisoner abuse is wrong, whether it is one case or one hundred.

Another dimension to this scandal not widely discussed is the "abuse" of women soldiers by their superiors in involving them in sexually suggestive acts with Guantánamo prisoners, as detailed in a Pentagon report released the week of July 10, 2005, on Guantánamo. Summarized by a *New York Times* editorial, the report included verification of the following incidents:

> There were several instances when female soldiers rubbed up against prisoners and touched them inappropriately. In April 2003, a soldier did that in a T-shirt after removing her uniform blouse . . . [another straddled a prisoner's lap], massaged his neck and shoulders, and "began to enter the personal space of the subject."

Incredibly, the Pentagon, the *Times* editorial noted, found none of this disturbing:

> The Pentagon seemed utterly unconcerned with the fact that women in uniform had been turned into sex workers at Guantánamo. The report's only conclusion was that whatever the female soldier might have done, it wasn't really a lap dance. Another instance, in which a female interrogator touched a prisoner with red ink and told him it was her menstrual blood, was judged

out of order—but only because the interrogator had cooked up the scheme to get back at the prisoner for spitting at her. The report said "retaliatory techniques" had to be approved in advance.[56]

Apparently the military views the detention of Iraqi children the same way. A June 2005 report by UNICEF (United Nations International Children's Education Fund) said that coalition forces led by the United States are in fact holding children under eighteen years of age deemed by the military to be a threat. Reports of abuse of these children are now being investigated by agencies such as Amnesty International. Coalition partner Denmark, along with its neighbor, Sweden, which has given tangential assistance to the war in Iraq, have both raised concerns about reported abuse of children prisoners.[57]

The "rightness" of seeking the truth regarding reports of this nature seems obvious, but the reality is that it takes courage born of personal integrity to speak to power, all the more so because power is so intoxicating. Even Billy Graham, a man of integrity, fell victim to the siren song of power during the presidency of Richard Nixon. He later admitted that he had made a mistake that resulted in his being used for Nixon's political advantage.[58] Living as we now do on the sidelines of political power, it may seem disingenuous for liberal Christians to point a finger at the Christian Right, who we believe are compromising their faith by playing with power. Would we be self-critical enough to see our seduction by it, were the roles reversed? Perhaps some of us would not, but history suggests some of us would.

Therein lies the difference between the two versions of Christianity. One of the strengths of modern fundamentalism is its solidarity, the likes of which are not to be found among liberals. But strengths are also weaknesses. Monolithic groups can be led in the wrong direction when the cause is presented as a moral crusade. Then conquering the enemy seems more important than recognizing internal dissent. Fundamentalist Christians seem to fear the influence of liberalism more than any concern they may have about compromising their own integrity. Success is measured by achieving the ultimate goal, which, in conjunction with political power, is always victory over the opponent. To defeat liberalism is the aim. Everything else is secondary.

Bigger Christianity disagrees. Nothing is more important than integrity, and no gain from having power can make up for the loss of it. But the damage this unholy alliance Christian fundamentalism has forged with political power around the nation extends to all Christians, especially since it has not gone unnoticed by the secular press. The *Times* editorial reported that

Religious conservatives have made their presence felt in so many other parts of the Bush administration, but they have been strangely quiet about these practices. And where are the members of Congress who wring their hands over the issue of women in combat? It's obvious that the Bush administration will never offer a real reckoning on the prisoner abuse, or that the Republican Party will demand one. But surely the dehumanizing of America's military women is a nonpartisan issue.

Until voices of dissent rise from the ranks of fundamentalists who have the courage to stand by their words, Bigger Christianity has no choice but to raise the issue of integrity about their inaction. Fundamentalists have aligned themselves with political power in an effort to gain "the world." But will they lose their soul in the process? For the sake of our own integrity, it is a question liberal Christians feel compelled to ask.

Prophetic vs. Patriotic

The other day my wife and I saw an SUV with six red, white, and blue magnetic ribbons plastered across the back and the sides. Inscribed on them were "Support our troops," "God bless America," "God bless the USA," and one that was difficult to read from my angle, but that I thought said, "We're the good guys." On that same day at a busy intersection we saw Iraqi War protestors on each corner. One older man had a sign on his front and back that said, "Grandfathers against the war."

These two experiences illustrate the difference between fundamentalist and liberal Christians—American flags made into vehicle ribbons over against homemade signs protesting war. As polls show the Iraqi War becoming more unpopular, each group seems to become more impassioned about its cause.[59] This dichotomy reflects a difference in emphasis. Fundamentalists focus on patriotism. Liberals focus on prophetic critique. Contrary to popular understanding, being "prophetic" as a person of faith is about *insight*, not foresight. It's not about what *will* happen; it's about what *is* happening. From this perspective, prophetic critique of government policies means evaluating public policy on the basis on truth and justice. Fundamentalism's concern for patriotism and Bigger Christianity's focus on prophetic critique point to a profound difference in the way each understands the role of Christianity in the world, especially since 9/11.

In the shadow of 9/11, liberal Christians are often accused of being unpatriotic because of our criticisms of the government on the Iraqi war, mistreatment of prisoners, environmental policies, tax cuts for the rich, and numerous other economic and social justice issues. It is not easy to challenge American policies in the face of the threat terrorism now poses. But for liberal Christians, neither is it easy to watch the carnage in Iraq and the continuing war in Afghanistan and say nothing about them. Or about oil companies that are financially rewarded by an energy bill that provides them with tax favors and profit windfalls at a time when they are showing record profits; or about drug companies that win approval of a Medicare drug benefit without having to offer competitive prices, while they are charging senior citizens the highest drug prices in the world; or about government officials who use selective data on climate change and then quit to go to work for the energy industry. Bigger Christianity believes that to remain uncritical is to become a partner in crime. As poet Wendell Berry has observed,

> the proposition that anything so multiple and large as a nation, or even a government, can be "good" is an insult to common sense. It is also danger-ous, because it precludes any attempt at self-criticism or self-correction; it precludes public dialogue. It leads us far indeed from the tradition of reli-gion and democracy that is intended to measure and so to sustain our efforts to be good. "There is none good but one, that is God," Christ said. Also, "He that is without sin among you, let him first cast a stone at her."[60]

Patriotism is a curious emotion. It has the power to unite and the power to divide. In the days following 9/11, all of us felt a sense of reverence and pride when we heard the national anthem played or joined in the singing of "Amer-ica, the Beautiful." But patriotism can be, and often is, used by those in power to squelch dissent. This danger is the reason Bigger Christianity seeks to maintain an appropriate distance from all politicians. Believing America is a great nation does not mean it is a flawless one. Nor does being patriotic mean that those flaws should be ignored or dismissed as insignificant in compari-son to other nations and in light of our many national attributes. If an indi-vidual is defensive when weaknesses are pointed out, we call it pride. If citizens respond in similar fashion when their country's flaws are exposed, we call it patriotism. It isn't, of course. It is pride, whose danger is exponen-tially greater than anything from which an individual may suffer. Govern-ments suppress their own people, promote class warfare, create economic oligarchies, and start wars.

The United States is no different from other nations in this regard. Our gov-ernment stole land and broke treaties with Native Americans. It started a war with Mexico for more land. It has allowed companies to work children and exploit workers. As a nation we went to war with ourselves because of the enslavement of our black citizens, then treated them as property after they won their freedom. We went to war in Viet Nam under false premises and have done so again in Iraq. Alongside these and other examples of misconduct are positive qualities such as a court system that seeks to treat all persons equally, an economic system that often rewards hard work, and a willingness to aid other nations in the fight against tyranny and economic repression. But there is no need or value to constantly remind ourselves of our good qualities as a nation. They speak for themselves. We point to national flaws, not to denigrate our country, but to make it stronger, in fact, to highlight the good side of who we are, as the following true story illustrates:

> The other day, though, I felt more self-conscious than usual. Every television in the gym highlighted some aspect of America's conflict with the Muslim world: the war in Iraq, allegations that American soldiers had desecrated the Koran, prisoner abuse at Guantánamo Bay, President Bush urging support of the Patriot Act. The stares just intensified my alienation as an Arab Muslim in what is supposed to be my country. I was not sure if the blood rushing to my head was caused by the elliptical trainer or by the news coverage.
>
> Frustrated and angry, I moved to another part of the gym. (Fatina Abdrabboh, student at the Kennedy School of Government at Harvard University)[61]

There are 10 million Arab and Muslim Americans in this country who move "to another part of the gym" daily. Bigger Christianity wonders how many Christians are among those who do the staring, and how many move with the Muslims as a sign of our common humanity. But Fatina's story didn't end with her moving. While on a treadmill, she dropped her keys, but she was so upset about what had happened, she continued to run. Moments later she felt a tap on the shoulder. When she turned, the man running behind her said, "Ma'am, you dropped your keys." He then went back to his treadmill. The man happened to be former vice president Al Gore. The impact of his gesture was powerful on her, as she described it:

> It was nothing more than a kind gesture, but at that moment Mr. Gore's act represented all that I yearned for—acceptance and acknowledgment. There in front of me, he stood for a part of America that has not made itself well known to 10 million Arab and Muslim-Americans, many of whom are becoming increasingly withdrawn and reclusive because of the everyday hostility they feel.
>
> It is up to us as Americans to change how the rest of the world views us by changing how we view some of our own citizens. Mr. Gore's act reminded me that rather than running away on my treadmill, I needed to keep my feet on the soil in this country. I left the gym with a renewed sense of spirit, reassured that I belong to America and that America belongs to me.

Most of us have not known the kind of prejudice Fatina and so many others like her experience. But all of us could make that part of America that Al Gore's gesture represented better known to those who have. Bigger Christianity believes that making the best part of who we are known is possible, because of prophetic ministry for the sake of the common good. Whoever said patriotism is the last resort of scoundrels was not cynical about ordinary citizens. He was cynical about governments, a distinction they have earned throughout history. Americans seem to have forgotten that our nation's founders were highly suspicious of the power of government to oppress its own people.

A genuine irony is that conservatives in general and fundamentalist Christians in particular distrust big government, but are willing to trust the current administration to do the right thing in all situations. Liberal Christians are not willing to give uncritical support to any administration at any time. We believe healthy skepticism makes for healthy patriotism. We believe that any form of government censorship is another name for propaganda. We believe the key to maintaining liberty and justice for all is to keep watch on the few who have power. What is encouraging is that the will to be prophetic is growing as Christians with a big faith become more alarmed by current policies. Two separate groups of faculty, staff, and alumni of Calvin College in Grand Rapids, Michigan, a college in the evangelical Christian tradition,[62] dared to speak a prophetic word to President Bush when it was announced that he would be the 2005 commencement speaker. One newspaper advertisement in part said,

> We are alumni, students, faculty and friends of Calvin College who are deeply troubled that you will be the commencement speaker at Calvin. In our view, the policies and actions of your administration, both domestically and internationally, over the past four years, violate many deeply held principles of Calvin College.[63]

Another ad, signed by a third of the Calvin faculty (some 130), read:

> As Christians, we are called to be peacemakers and to initiate war only as a last resort. We believe your administration has launched an unjust and unjustified war in Iraq.

"By their deeds ye shall know them," reads the paid advertisement, quoting the Bible.

> Your deeds, Mr. President—neglecting the needy to coddle the rich, desecrating the environment, and misleading the country into war—do not exemplify the faith we live by.
> Moreover, many of your supporters are using religion as a weapon to

divide our nation and advance a narrow partisan agenda. . . . We urge you not to use Calvin College as a platform to advance policies that violate the school's religious principles.[64]

Most striking in these statements was the reference to Bush supporters "using religion as a weapon to divide our nation and advance a narrow partisan agenda." It would require an intentional blindness not to see how true this is. And that is what prophetic utterance is—having the courage to say what most people with sufficient courage would also say. Undaunted by the prospect of being called unpatriotic, these brave Christians chose to follow in the tradition of biblical prophets anyway. And they did so as a community of Christians, not as individuals, providing greater credibility for their perspective and insight.

As you might expect, the criticism was swift in coming. On his web blog, Al Mohler, the Christian fundamentalist president of Southern Baptist Theological Seminary, Louisville, Kentucky, wrote:

> This is a sad spectacle and an inappropriate politicization of an academic ceremony. Without even addressing the over-the-top language and claims made in the statement [hardly worthy of serious political engagement], the protest should be an embarrassment to all who supported it. No political leader is above criticism, and President Bush's policies—like that of every President—draw both praise and lamentation. But the President of the United States is more than a political leader, he represents the nation as Chief Executive. President Bush did not go to Calvin to deliver a political speech, but to take part in a formal academic ceremony. Even the local newspaper saw the issue more clearly than the childish faculty members who staged the protest. As the paper editorialized, a graduation ceremony is no place for this kind of protest.[65]

The naiveté in suggesting any president would deliver a "nonpolitical" commencement address aside, prophets do not wait for an "appropriate" time to speak. In the eyes of established powers, there is no such time. In a post- 9/11 America in which national leaders say we are engaged in a war on terror that by its very nature has no end, this is especially true. The witness of biblical prophets such as Isaiah and Jeremiah reminds us that there may be no time more appropriate than this to speak prophetically. This war on terror, as well as the war in Iraq, like all wars consumes vital resources that are necessary for our nation to keep faith with social responsibilities. Human casualties are the worst aspect of war, but the financial drain is also staggering. Iraq, for example, is costing five billion dollars a month, an amount too large for most of us to comprehend. Political leaders say we will spend whatever it takes to win, but they seldom have the same resolve when it comes to social needs. A prophetic faith speaks against such misplaced priorities and misused resources.

In today's environment, the prophetic voice of Bigger Christianity also serves as a guardian of liberty. The news media once carried this responsibility, but with the emergence of media conglomerates, the free press has become captive to "the bottom line." *Atlantic* magazine correspondent James Fallows says news reporting has stopped being a profession, and is now a business. As in other businesses, the priority is profit, not news. And the two are often in conflict.[66] Under a court order, for example, Norman Pearlstein, editorial director of *Time* magazine, agreed to turn over the notes of *Time* reporter Matt Cooper in the case of columnist Robert Novak's leaking of the name of Valerie Plame as a CIA operative. Thus far special prosecutor Patrick Fitzgerald has secured a grand jury indictment against Lewis "Scooter" Libby, former chief of staff for Vice President Dick Cheney. Before the indictment, *New York Times* reporter Judith Miller spent eighty-five days in jail for refusing to testify before the grand jury.

In an interview with Wolf Blitzer,[67] journalists Bob Woodward and Carl Bernstein of Watergate's Deep Throat fame were both appalled at *Time* magazine's decision, Miller's jailing, and pressure from Fitzgerald on several reporters to reveal their sources. In his book *The Secret Man*, which is the story of FBI agent Mark Felt admitting to being Watergate's "Deep Throat," "the secret man," Woodward asserts: "It is critical that confidential sources feel they would be protected for life. There needed to be a model out there where people could come forward or speak when contacted, knowing they would be protected."

Blitzer asked Woodward if he thought *Time* magazine's actions fit that model. He replied that he did not know enough about Cooper's role in the Plame case to answer the question. But, he continued, he could not imagine his former *Washington Post* editor, Ben Bradlee, turning over his and Bernstein's notes. "We can't say on the air what Bradlee would have said to them." Later in the interview, Woodward said to Blitzer, "We better wake up to what's going on in the seriousness of the assault on the First Amendment that's taking place right before our eyes."

Still not satisfied, Blitzer pushed Bernstein to say whether or not he thought Pearlstein was wrong to turn over Cooper's notes. Bernstein answered that while he respected Pearlstein, he thought he had made a mistake, at which point Woodward added:

It's undermining the core function in journalism. If the people out there who watch television, read the newspapers, want public relations experts and spokespersons to define all of the news, fine, because that's exactly what's going to happen.

Since that interview, Woodward himself has come under criticism for not disclosing to his executive editor, Leonard Downie Jr., that a senior administration official had also told him that Plame was a CIA agent nearly a month before Novak wrote about it. This revelation can only deepen the public's suspicion and cynicism that attracting the largest possible audience in pursuit of the biggest possible profits is the primary goal of the media today, and that questioning government action is no real concern at all.

In an environment of a cowed media, the need for people of faith to demand and seek the truth from government leaders at all levels is acute. When a free press has been bought off, Christianity as a representative of justice and fairness has an obligation to ensure that government claims are grounded in truth, rather than serving simply as an instrument of propaganda. Wendell Berry reminds us that it was Jefferson himself who "justified general education by the obligation of citizens to be critical of their government: 'for nothing can keep it right but their own vigilant and distrustful superintendence.'" Berry understands this obligation to mean that "an inescapable requirement of true patriotism, love for one's land, is a vigilant distrust of any determinative power, elected or unelected, that may preside over it."[68]

Wendell Berry is not the only artist who understands the role of vigilant distrust of power in preserving democracy. Well-known graphic artist Milton Glaser sponsored an exhibit to promote a book of over 200 artists called "Design of Dissent." The purpose of these provocative images, Glaser said, is to question authority and seek to speak truth to power. When asked by David Brancaccio during an interview on a July 1, 2005, broadcast of *NOW* what it was about the media landscape in 2005 that provoked these images of dissent, he replied:

> Well, there's a real problem with the media landscape and you know certainly as well as anybody else which is that the media in general has become exceedingly passive in regard to its response to government. If we don't have a vigorous questioning, aggressive journalistic community and mythology, democracy itself is in great jeopardy.
>
> You really have seen that the last few years, that the whole democratic underpinnings of America have been threatened by a very weak journalistic community that simply has not been willing to take on the President or the existing government.

This particular administration, of course, is not unique in its desire to shield itself from criticism and exposure. What is different is a media more concerned about profit than democracy. In this new environment, liberal Christians can—and must—join this dissent through the prophetic vocation that is ours to fulfill. It is the way of Bigger Christianity.

Peace-filled vs. Militaristic

"Blessed are the peacemakers" is as basic to the Christian message as it gets. The Greek word for "blessed" means "fortunate, well off, happy." Jesus says "peacemakers" are the people who "will be called (named, hailed as) children (sons or kin) of God" (Matthew 5:9). This is a straightforward statement that seems to assert that peacemaking is a Christian vocation. It is not limited to Christians, but it is endemic to being Christian. In short, a non-peacemaking Christian is an oxymoron. It is inconceivable that a Jesus follower could be a proponent of war. Peace and war are opposites. Nothing in history suggests the latter maintains the former. Making war does not make for peace. To believe it does is to perpetuate "a hallowed absurdity."[69] The true reality about war is that its end always leaves behind the seeds of another. "Violence begets violence" is an axiom confirmed by human experience.

All Christians believe in peace. Indeed, all sane people do. But most of us nuance our commitment to it because we suspect that peace is an ideal more suited for a perfect world and that war is a weapon of self-preservation needed in the real world. Again, history seems to confirm this as wisdom. How would Hitler have been stopped had the Allies not gone to war? The "appeasement" of British Prime Minister Neville Chamberlain to Hitler prior to his invasion of Poland is a sobering reminder of the consequences of peacemaking naiveté. Theologians such as Reinhold Niebuhr have made persuasive arguments that Christian pacifism takes the power of collective evil too lightly. Niebuhr also believed much of this naiveté stemmed from the mistaken assumption that all violence was intrinsically unethical. Even peaceful efforts can have negative consequences, he noted; for example, Gandhi's boycott of British cotton resulted in undernourishment of Manchester children, and the blockade by Allies in World War I caused the death of German children.[70]

Niebuhr did not advocate war. His concern was the middle ground between the religious moralist who insists reason and conscience make for peace and the political realist who believes violence is the primary means of preserving social order. It is this middle ground that makes Niebuhr's insights relevant today. He argued:

Equal justice is the most rational ultimate objective for society. If this conclusion is correct, a social conflict which aims at greater equality has a moral
justification which must be denied to efforts which aim at the perpetuation
of privilege. A war for the emancipation of a nation, a race or a class is thus
placed in a different moral category from the use of power for the perpetuation of imperial rule or class dominance.[71]

This principle could be used to justify most wars. But Niebuhr went on to
highlight Gandhi's nonviolent spirit as a guide to social resistance. Unwilling
to say violence is intrinsically unethical in a just cause, Niebuhr nonetheless
saw the need for a spirit of moral goodwill even in conflict.[72] This was not for
him an arbitrary distinction. Niebuhr quotes Gandhi's explanation of his support for the British during World War I:

Non-violence works in a most mysterious manner. Often a man's actions
defy analysis in terms of non-violence; equally often his actions may bear
the appearance of violence when he is absolutely non-violent in the highest
sense of the term, and is subsequently found to be so. All I can claim for my
conduct is that I was, in that instance cited, actuated in the interest of nonviolence. There was no thought of sordid national or other interests.[73]

Niebuhr understood Gandhi to be saying that "even violence is justified
if it proceeds from perfect goodwill. But he is equally insistent that nonviolence is usually the better method of expressing goodwill."[74]

Possessing a nonviolent spirit while engaging in war is not as difficult to
judge or trust as it may appear to be. Our failure to stop the genocide in
Rwanda in the 1990s and the U.S. attack on Iraq in 2003 illustrate the significance of the difference. Tutsi warriors were openly slaughtering Hutu men,
women, and children by the thousands. The United Nations did nothing
because the United States and the majority of member states blocked it from
doing anything. More than a million people were killed by the world's inaction. In this instance, Bigger Christianity would agree that nonviolence was
the morally wrong thing to do.

The U.S. invasion of Iraq was based on the assertion that Saddam Hussein
posed an imminent threat to the security of our nation. That turned out not to
be the case, and there is mounting evidence that the books were cooked to support the case that he was. But even had he been such a threat, it would have
been difficult to prove that Niebuhr's "greater equality" was in play at the
time. The Bush administration might have been able to argue that the invasion
was morally right because the emancipation of a nation was at stake, as it did
after the case for weapons of mass destruction evaporated. But the emancipation argument also has problems, since we initiated the conflict from the out-

side rather than coming to the aid of rebel forces within Iraq. At no time, though, have our leaders demonstrated the key element in Niebuhr's argument for justified violence: nothing suggests our leaders possessed then or now a nonviolent spirit, a spirit of goodwill. On the contrary, they speak of the war in phrases like "Bring it on."

Herein lies the reason for Bigger Christianity's resistance to the Iraqi War and the way in which the war on terrorism is being waged. A violent spirit within the nation and its leaders seems to have driven, and to be still driving, our actions. It's a kind of "payback time" mentality for what "they" did to us—except the Iraqis didn't do it. Using the Niebuhrian principle that violence is justified in a cause for greater equality or the emancipation of a nation or people, liberal Christians oppose the war in Iraq and the conduct of the war on terrorism because of the obvious absence of a spirit of goodwill. The spirit of nonviolence—which could prevent us from becoming like those who flew the planes into the towers—is the higher righteousness Jesus talked about. It is the blessed state of being a peacemaker of the heart, fully cognizant that nonviolence is always the preferred way to spread goodwill and peace.

A militaristic attitude is something not distinctive of the modern world. It's as old as humanity and has an insatiable appetite. It should be no surprise that state and federal budgets reflect waning support for social programs that express a desire for a greater equality among our people. Increases in military spending, coupled with tax cuts benefiting the very wealthy in our nation, inevitably mean less money for everything else. They also underscore the extent to which we as a people have lost our way as a reasonable, civil culture. The real culture of death we have in America today is a culture of violence. As a people, we have come to believe we can live by the sword without dying by it.

When David Letterman asked former president Bill Clinton what he thought about the war in Iraq, he said that it didn't matter now why we were there, that we had to stay and make it a success. For liberal Christians, the idea that the reasons for going to war don't matter after the war has started is morally repugnant. By that standard, world leaders could wage war any time they chose, in the expectation that all will be well that ends well. The first obligation of a leader, to protect the nation's security, includes the solemn responsibility to put no soldier in harm's way unless there is a compelling reason for doing so. In this respect, Iraq is precisely what Viet Nam was. President Lyndon Johnson turned that conflict into a futile and bloody war on false pretenses. President Bush has done the same thing in Iraq, and in the process has made "being there" the justification for continuing the war.

The problem with this point of view is that, like Viet Nam, this is a war that cannot be "won" in the conventional sense of that term. Urban warfare is not battlefield warfare. Staying the course will mean thousands more military and civilian deaths, with the likelihood that at some point in the future our nation will realize what we finally understood in Viet Nam—that this kind of war has no end. We will then leave Iraq without "victory," raising the specter that all the killing was ultimately in vain. Even American military leaders have said that this is a war that cannot be won on the battlefield, that it will take a political solution to bring it to an end.

The very least that can be said at this point is that the war has become a flashpoint of public controversy even among those who once supported it. In November of 2005 Pennsylvania Congressman John Murtha, a hawkish Democrat, sent shock waves through the capital when he held a news conference to announce that he believed the time had come when President Bush should establish a timetable for the withdrawal of U.S. troops. Before Murtha's change of mind, John Deutch, deputy secretary of defense from 1994 to 1995, director of central intelligence from 1995 to 1996, and currently a professor of chemistry at MIT, had suggested that the problem we are facing is grounded in confusion about the way in which the American military must function in today's international environment:

> We should not shirk from quick military action for the purpose of saving lives that are in immediate danger. For example, the decision not to intervene early to prevent mass murder in Rwanda was a major failure. But we should not be lured into intervention that has as its driving purpose the replacement of despotic regimes with systems of government more like our own. It is not that the purpose is unworthy, but rather that it is unlikely to succeed. . . . Reshaping our military to take on the activities that the Pentagon euphemistically calls "stability and security" operations will come at a cost—both in terms of potentially compromising the war-fighting capacity of our troops and in diverting the resources needed to support the civic action that underlies nation-building.[75]

Liberal Christians see opposing the war in Iraq as an example of the need for all Christians to do more than give lip service to peacemaking. We believe building a peaceable kingdom here on earth is a sacred work. As the children of God, we believe peacemaking is the work of God we must do here on earth. But we are not naive about the task. Bigger Christianity has no illusion we can convince political leaders not to go to war. We do believe, however, that we can build enough public sentiment for peace that they will go to war only as a last resort. We also believe we can expose the lack of political will to find a nonviolent solution. Christians do have the power to raise awareness of the benefits of peace, so that a skeptical public, aware that history is replete with examples of wars beginning without just cause, will scrutinize any reason for going to war.

In addition, we believe that justice demands that everyone bear the burden of war, including the war in Iraq. This was not done in Viet Nam, when minorities and middle-class soldiers died by the thousands, while draft exemptions allowed thousands of others, especially the affluent, to avoid going. The absence of a draft now does not mean, however, that the burden of fighting the war on terrorism cannot be shared more broadly. Just after 9/11, Pulitzer Prize–winning author Thomas Friedman suggested what he called a patriot tax, a $1-per-gallon gasoline tax that would focus attention on the need for all Americans to end our love affair with gas-guzzling vehicles to reduce our dependence on foreign oil. Further, the tax would have created a superfund to support research in innovative energy alternatives. Such a tax would have been felt by everyone, as all just taxes should be. Every moment we stood at the pump, we would be reminded of our contribution to the war on terror. But, as he notes, the opportunity was missed. Instead, the American people were advised to go shopping. But the lesson is worth remembering. There are numerous ways the burden of war can and should be borne by the whole nation.

This kind of education is the work of peacemakers. Being a Bigger Christian means embracing it as a vocation, acknowledging the temptations to violence in our own lives, while remaining committed to nurturing a nonviolent spirit. When it comes to nonviolence, an example is worth a thousand words. Liberal Christians must live peaceably to teach the Bigger Christianity we believe in. We must be the kind of people whose attitudes and actions naturally invite people of goodwill to a higher standard of conduct than striking when struck. Peacemaking is not irrelevant to an age of terrorism. It is what Christians believe is the one hope we have to survive in a world that has become smaller than it ever has been. As Stanley Hauerwas has written, "nonviolence is not just one implication among others that can be drawn from our Christian beliefs; it is at the very heart of our understanding of God."[76]

Of course, peacemaking seems weak in the face of the power of governments to wage war. But once in a while something unexpected happens that reminds us that it is not as weak as many of us believe and that, against great odds, those who witness for peace have an impact. One such example occurred in the summer of 2005. Cindy Sheehan, a grief-stricken mother whose twenty-four-year-old son Casey was killed in Iraq, set up camp on the road leading to President Bush's Crawford, Texas, ranch. She vowed to stay as long as the president was on vacation there, or until he agreed to meet with her to explain why her son had to die in a war she believed should not have been fought. Soon other grieving parents joined her, and her encampment took on a life of its own. The media began to pay attention to her protest. For two weeks "Camp Casey," so named after her son, was in the news. It is possible that when the story of the Iraq War is written, Cindy Sheehan's peace protest will be seen as the catalyst that began the erosion of public support for it. An incident that took place illustrates why.

A man in a huge diesel pickup truck rumbled into camp facing the tents of the protestors, and then sat without moving for what seemed to everyone watching a very long time. Finally, Ann Wright, the main organizer of camp activities and a former U.S. diplomat, approached the truck and met the driver. He turned out to be a father whose son had been killed in Iraq. He disagreed with Cindy Sheehan's protest, he said, but he wanted to know if his son's name was on one of the crosses the group had placed along the road to commemorate the American soldiers who had died in Iraq. They called it the Arlington West Cemetery. Ann invited the man to walk the rows of crosses and find his son's name. When he did, he and Ann sat down in front of it, wrapped their arms around each other, and wept. Later, the man shared a beer with Cindy and told her he loved her.[77]

In that moment, peace had won a victory. In pitching her tent on the Crawford ranch road, Cindy Sheehan managed to do what no one else had been able to do up to that moment. She forced a nation to see the human face of the Iraq war, and Bigger Christianity quietly prayed, "Blessed are the peacemakers, for they possess the power to open the eyes of all of us to the will of God on earth."

Stewards vs. Owners

Our family lives on a busy street that runs in front of a high school. Almost daily we stop our car in the driveway to get out and pick up discarded bottles, cigarette packs, food wrappers, bags of all sizes, school announcement sheets, and other garbage that people—especially high school students—throw out of their passing cars. That people are stewards of the earth, not its owners, is a no-brainer. But when it comes to remembering "The earth is the LORD's and all that is in it, the world, and those who live in it" (Psalm 24:1), apparently not everyone has a brain.

There is nothing new about environmental abuse. As a nation we came perilously close to killing the Great Lakes, all the shellfish in the Chesapeake Bay in Virginia, and thousands of lakes and streams across the country—along with poisoning the air we breathe. Environmentalists finally got the nation's attention in the 1960s and the cleanup began. But we have apparently run out of "energy" for preserving the environment. "Greens" are looked upon as liberals who care more about spotted owls than about people who need the jobs that protecting owls would take away. What is astounding is that Christian fundamentalism has joined the chorus of criticism that argues environmentalists have gone too far. Emission standards for coal-fired power plants need to be relaxed, they say. Nuclear power plants need to be built, despite the fact that after thirty years of trying, no suitable way to dispose of nuclear waste has been found. Fundamentalists even supported General Motors in its fight against higher mileage standards so it would not have to spend money modifying the SUVs and Humvees that were selling as fast as they came off the assembly line. Fundamentalists didn't launch a television campaign in support of this shortsighted lobbying effort. Rather, their endorsement came indirectly through support for the Bush administration's environmental policies that supported General Motors, along with whatever the oil industry needed to exploit oil reserves in Alaska. The lone voice of opposition to this lobbying campaign was that of the "greens" who fundamentalists believe are part of a great liberal conspiracy to destroy America's economic superiority in the world.

Bigger Christianity sees the issue from a different perspective. It believes Christianity has an incredible opportunity to speak on behalf of responsible stewardship of the planet in ways that challenge the solipsistic, self-centered thinking that is driving the destruction of the environment. Without the intricate balances necessary for life on earth to continue, nothing else matters very much. It will all come down on our heads in a way that will have everyone wondering how the human race could have been so shortsighted. Frankly, "shortsighted" is a word too kind for what some corporations are doing, chief among them the Fortune 500, multinational chemical company W. R. Grace. The uncovering of W. R. Grace's willingness to put people at risk by poisoning the environment began when three-year-old Jimmy Anderson got sick. Months of tests finally led to the bad news that Jimmy had lymphocytic leukemia. Hearing the news, some of Anne and Charles Carner's neighbors began to bring in casseroles and baked goods. One of them, Kay Bolster, mentioned to Anne that her neighbors on either side also had sons who had been diagnosed with leukemia. Anne phoned one of the mothers, Joan Zona, who invited Anne for coffee. The two grieving mothers talked about the coincidence of four cases of lymphocytic leukemia in the same neighborhood, how difficult it was to face the news about their sons, and their doubts and hopes about the future. Both women knew talking helped, so they agreed to meet again soon.

What followed from their first community meeting was the slow but steady unfolding of the extent to which city wells had been poisoned and the workers at Grace's tanning factory exposed to toxic chemicals. Finally they persuaded a young attorney named Jan Schlictmann to take their case and filed suit against W. R. Grace and its chemical supplier, Beatrice Foods Company. It was the beginning of a firsthand encounter with corporate giants with unlimited resources, masterfully using legal maneuvering to counter charges against them. They also witnessed the rulings of the presiding judge, Walter J. Skinner, who seemed determined to tilt the playing field in favor of Grace and Beatrice Foods. The sordid details of this tragic miscarriage of justice for residents of Woburn, Massachusetts, are detailed in Jonathan Harr's book *A Civil Action*.[78] But the real point for our purposes is that some companies will stop at nothing to make money, even if it means destroying the environment and putting whole communities in jeopardy. W. R. Grace was involved in other lawsuits similar to the Woburn case and in 2001 filed for bankruptcy protection from a suit filed by workers of a Minnesota asbestos manufacturing plant it once owned.

Bigger Christianity wants to know why there is no moral outrage among fundamentalist Christians over this kind of behavior. The Woburn case is one of hundreds of true stories of companies treating the environment as if they own it and of the dire consequences that have resulted from their actions. The silence of fundamentalists is appalling. Christians of every stripe believe the world belongs to God. Nothing should make us hesitant to speak on behalf of a world that has no voice other than ours. In chapter 1, we wondered out loud why all Christians would not call themselves "liberal," given the marvelous meaning of the word. In addition, we wonder why all Christians would not want to call themselves "greens," or "environmentalists," given the urgent need for humanity to learn the difference between ownership and stewardship.

I want to suggest six elemental convictions about our relationship to the earth that are reasons enough for any Christian to want to be an environmentalist. To take a page from Robert Fulghum,[79] these are things we learned—or should have learned—in kindergarten: (1) we didn't make it; (2) we don't own it; (3) we should be careful how we use it; (4) we should not use more of it than we need; (5) we should clean up after ourselves; (6) we should want to leave it for others to enjoy.

The questions God posed to Job (Job 38:4–11) seem to speak directly to the issue of creation and ownership. The words below sound very much like God saying, "You didn't make it, and you don't own it."

> "Where were you when I laid the foundation of the earth?
>   Tell me, if you have understanding.
> Who determined its measurements—surely you know!
>   Or who stretched the line upon it?
> On what were its bases sunk,
>   or who laid its cornerstone

when the morning stars sang together
    and all the heavenly beings shouted for joy?
Or who shut in the sea with doors
    when it burst out from the womb?—
when I made the clouds its garment,
    and thick darkness its swaddling band,
and prescribed bounds for it,
    and set bars and doors,
and said, 'Thus far shall you come, and no farther,
    and here shall your proud waves be stopped'?"

If we didn't make the earth and don't own it, it naturally follows that we should be careful about how we use it. When I borrow anything that belongs to someone else, I take extra care in the way I use it. It is not overly simplistic to suggest human beings need this kind of attitude toward God's creation. This would include an awareness of the need for stewardship of resources, so that we will not mess up or leave without cleaning up after ourselves on a personal and corporate basis.

If we practice the first five convictions, number six will take care of itself. Unfortunately, Christianity's traditional teaching of dominion over the earth works against the simple convictions above. If you believe dominion means control, occupation begins to look a lot like ownership. But no one is arrogant enough to come right out and say it; so this attitude gets couched in other language, such as concern for economic development. Environmental concerns, it is said, must be balanced by economic realities. But even on the face of it, the expediency of this argument is apparent. If it costs too much to require coal-burning power plants to meet stricter sulfuric acid standards, future generations will have to pay the price by breathing poisoned air. That hardly squares with how liberal Christians understand the biblical message.

Stewardship vs. ownership is such a simple concept to grasp. That may be where the problems start. Love is also a simple concept, but we all know what happens when people try to put it into practice. But, in truth, failure to love has to do less with ability to love than with a lack of will. All of us can love better than we do. Environmental stewardship is no different. We can do better than we do. The fault does not lie in the human ability to make progress while preserving the integrity of land, water, and air. The problem is an absence of the will to do so. Mistreating the environment is like mistreating a person. It is an act of volition, which means we are responsible for our actions. Environmental stewardship is also like love in that you cannot make someone do it. Laws can prevent abuse from going unpunished, but they do not prevent it from happening in the first place. The will has to come from within. But until it does, laws must protect the public interest. There is ample evidence that "voluntary compliance" is used by industries as an opportunity to ignore EPA standards.

In the spring of 2005, the Environmental Protection Agency issued new guidelines for assessing cancer risk from chemical pollutants. According to the Natural Resources Defense Council (NRDC), these guidelines will give industry opportunities to stifle safeguards that protect children. The guidelines acknowledge that children under two years of age are ten times more likely to get cancer from certain chemicals than adults who are similarly exposed. In spite of this fact, the White House Office of Management and Budget inserted language in the guidelines that make it easy for industry to block EPA from enforcing them when assessing cancer-causing chemicals. "The White House decided it was more important to protect the chemical industry than protect our kids from cancer," said Dr. Jennifer Sass, a senior scientist with the NRDC's environmental health program. "The White House took what would have been strong guidelines to protect our children from cancer and turned them into an industry punching bag. Chemical companies will be able to pummel any new safeguard to death. The chemical industry wins, our children lose."[80]

Bigger Christianity doesn't need coaxing to embrace standards to protect our children and the earth they will inherit. Profits are important, but not at the expense of the world of which we are called to be stewards. Liberal Christians believe an attitude of ownership toward the earth is idolatrous. Believing in God means accepting the human role of stewards. The environmental mantra of every steward should be, "We didn't make, we don't own it, and we ought to act like it."

When I was much younger, the threat of a nuclear holocaust hung over the world as a potential mushroom cloud. Hardly a day went by that we were not reminded of the fact that the United States and the Soviet Union possessed the power to destroy the earth several times over. The end of the Cold War did not eliminate this threat, but it certainly made it less inevitable. But in reality the world is already being destroyed. The worst part is that its subtlety makes the threat seem less urgent. It's as if termites are eating away the foundations of the earth, but few people are paying attention, and those who are attentive are being ignored. In the future, humanity may face the inevitable truth that we in fact have been the termites and that we have destroyed ourselves.

This sounds like doomsday talk, doesn't it? For that, Bigger Christianity makes no apology. The dangers we face are real. Polar icecaps are melting, sending unusual amounts of fresh water into the oceans' currents. Salt water is heavy and sinks. Fresh water is light and floats. As salt water is pushed farther down by this influx of fresh water, ocean currents are altered. That in turn affects thousands of other things. None of this is theoretical. It is happening now, and it is very real.

Environmental stewardship is not a game, nor is it optional. Rejecting the attitude of ownership that the Western world has allowed to guide its behavior and policies is literally a matter of life or death. That is about as moral as any issue gets. Yet not a single fundamentalist Web site I have found devotes any attention to environmental stewardship. Indeed, it seems quite odd that fundamentalists who want to push teaching of creationism in schools are silent in light of what is happening. Liberal Christians may not do enough to practice good stewardship, but we believe "green" is a very "Christian" color to be.

Eradication vs. Gradualism

Poverty is humanity's most acute problem. It kills more people daily than any other crisis we face. Every day 20,000 people die of hunger and its related diseases. Eight million will perish this year. According to scholar and writer Jeffrey Sachs, they die "in hospital wards that lack drugs, in villages that lack antimalarial bed nets, in houses that lack safe drinking water. They die namelessly, without public comment."[81] The World Bank, he notes, estimates that 1.1 billion people live in extreme poverty, most of them in Asia and Africa. "Extreme poverty" means living on less than a dollar a day. But these people won't live. They will die. The world's poor who manage to survive live in moderate and relative poverty that enslaves close to half of the world's six billion people.

What makes this tragedy worse is that it is preventable. Sachs documents that survival for these people is possible, even reasonable, because of the existence of "known, proven, reliable and appropriate technologies and interventions."[82] Governments in countries where extreme poverty is common often have stood and often do stand in the way of such help. But Western nations have leverage that has been and can be used to ensure that starving people get food and water and that the long-term work of helping poor nations boost agriculture, improve basic health, invest in education, generate electrical power, and provide clean water and sanitation can expand exponentially. The lack of knowledge, technology, or local government support is not the reason little is being done to end systemic poverty and hunger. Rather, the reason is a *lack of will*. The developed nations of the world are signatories to the Monterrey Consensus, a product of the 2002 United Nations conference that brought together representatives from governments and businesses to explore ways to finance global development. This noble cause is expressed in the first paragraph of the Consensus: "Our goal is to eradicate poverty, achieve sustained economic growth and promote sustainable development as we advance to a fully inclusive and equitable global economic system."[83]

As a participant in this joint effort to mobilize international cooperation and resources for eradicating poverty, the United States pledged 0.7 percent of its GNP to this end. As of the fall of 2005, we have failed to follow through on this commitment. Sadly, this is a common practice among developed countries. Agreements to confront social ills are signed without subsequent actions being taken. Our own government justifies its inaction with the excuse that its work to spread democracy and capitalism around the world in the long run is the most effective way to help the poor of the world invest in their own future. Meanwhile, the holocaust that is called poverty continues.

Liberal Christians believe compassion is the way of Jesus. It needs no adjective. Compassionate "conservative" or compassionate "liberal" puts the focus on the wrong quality. Followers of Jesus are compassionate. We love the way he loved. We give away compassion with no strings attached. People who are poor and needy do not have to deserve our compassion. We share it without qualifications or obligations. While liberal and fundamentalist Christians agree that compassion is a virtue, we differ on how to put it into action. Their refusal to be critical of our government's failure to direct resources to confront the crisis of poverty and hunger is a de facto acceptance of the policy of gradualism to help the world's poorest of the poor.

Liberal Christians choose to call for immediate action. This is a moral issue. But, as it turns out, our government's lack of will to act now to eradicate hunger is actually a stinging indictment of us as a people. Nothing changes, Sachs says, because there is "no political fallout domestically" over this lack of will.[84] With the chance to eliminate extreme poverty, we have a government that procrastinates because we as a people are willing to tolerate this kind of government. Spreading democracy and capitalism may be worthy goals, but children and adults will needlessly die before that happens.

Bigger Christianity is unwilling to invest in such a futuristic hope when the problem of global hunger is solvable now. Nor are we willing to sit by without criticizing the misplaced priorities our nation's inaction represents. This is a moral failure of epic proportions. We frequently hear political and religious leaders speak of America as the greatest nation on earth. But in the face of the eight million deaths that occur from hunger annually, when we could lead the world in preventing them but don't, what is the measure of "greatness" we have in mind? How "great" is a nation that spends 30 billion dollars a year on pet care while global poverty kills millions of people? Moreover, because poverty is a breeding ground for social unrest around the world, what is the measure of our collective "wisdom" in ignoring it as we fight the war on terrorism? Shortsightedness is part of the human condition, but in this instance the consequences are catastrophic.

When Jesus said the poor would always be with us (Matthew 26:11), he was responding to the reality of the first-century world. At the beginning of the twenty-first century, these same words carry a different message. No longer are the poor with us because we lack the power to change their circumstances. They are with us because we do not possess a sense of moral urgency to demand that governments do what needs to be done to end poverty. Christians are the ones who should feel the brunt of Jesus' words most acutely. We should know and do better. Churches could set an example for our government to follow. That we don't suggests the modern church may be the rich ruler who needs to sell everything it possesses and give it to the poor as a sign of our willingness truly to follow Jesus (Luke 18:18–23). In the face of the solvable problem of world poverty, the millions of dollars being spent on buildings dedicated to God is the modern equivalent of European cathedrals being built on the backs of village peasants. If we do not have the will to sell "everything," we could at least have the will to do better than we are doing now. Governments have no reason to listen to the voice of a Christian community that willfully refuses to practice what it preaches. Compassion is the way of Jesus. Bigger Christianity believes that putting the necessary resources to work in eradicating poverty and hunger is how it needs to be practiced.

God Bless The World vs. God Bless America

The contrast in the heading above summarizes the differences between small Christianity and the Bigger Christianity we have been discussing. Bigger Christianity believes God belongs to no one but is One to whom all people belong. Small Christianity speaks and acts as if God favors the United States over *all other* nations. We have already noted that the "divine destiny" notions that abounded in early America are still prevalent, often expressed in the historical revisionist claim that ours is a Christian nation. Thus, in the scheme of things, Americans are "the good guys." But our focus here is not the presumptuousness of that way of thinking. Rather, it is on the word "bless." The phrase is actually a prayer.

To ask God to bless a nation or all nations is a theological affirmation that God exists. Bigger Christianity thinks this is a life-changing statement of faith. Truly believing God exists changes your entire worldview. No longer can you think or act as if your life is your own, that your needs matter more than those of others, or that you are the center of your own life. Bigger Christianity believes in a sovereign God who is free from human manipulation or control. This means Christians who pray for God's blessing on the nation are first obligated to be discriminating about what we are asking God to bless. Is it the 85,000 tons of bombs we dropped on Iraq in the first Gulf War, which hit not only military targets, but schools, homes, and mosques? Were we singing "God Bless America" as Colin Powell, when asked how many Iraqis had been killed by what some have characterized as an American "blitzkrieg," responded, "Frankly, that's a number that doesn't interest me very much"?[85] Are we asking God to bless our war against "terrorists" in Iraq now, so we won't have to fight them here, even though we are killing Iraqi children by the thousands in the process? Or are we asking God to bless the dissident voices that challenge the morality of our actions and question the rightness of our policies? Do we want God to bless the injustice of a fraction of the world's population using an excess of the world's resources or the attitude that we have the right to impose our will on the rest of the world because we are the only nuclear superpower of the twenty-first century? Indeed, what are we asking God to bless?

Military Families Speak Out is an organization of people who have relatives or loved ones in the military but who are also opposed to the war in Iraq. Formed in November 2002, the group is composed of some 2,200 military families throughout the United States and in other countries who have dared to speak out against the war in Iraq. They describe their purpose this way:

> We have both a special need and a unique role to play in speaking out against war in Iraq. It is our loved ones who are, or have been, or will be on the battlefront. It is our loved ones who are risking injury and death. It is our loved ones who are returning scarred from their experiences. It is our loved ones who will have to live with the injuries and deaths among innocent Iraqi civilians.[86]

Instead of falling lockstep behind the war, these patriotic Americans understand that they carry a special responsibility to follow their conscience. I do not know their religious ties, but it is likely that many of them are guided by faith in taking the stand they have taken. In return they have been criticized and demonized. One caller on a radio talk show commented that he "loathed their existence."

The courage of these military families in challenging the moral basis of this war is an example of the kind of attitude toward the government all Christians would do well to consider. It is precisely their position as families of soldiers that leads them to speak as they are doing. Because we are Christian, we resist aligning ourselves uncritically with this nation and its policies. Liberal Christians ask God to bless the world and not just America. We trust in the God who is owned by no nation and plays no favorites in the world of human affairs. The world belongs to God, and God has already bestowed the blessing of life on the world. To ask for God to bless the world is in reality a request for wisdom in choosing life over death. That is an appropriate prayer to pray because it confesses that God has already set before all people the choice of life and death. The world must now choose the direction to follow. One way leads to life, the other to death. This is not a divine judgment. It is a consequence of our freedom to choose. Without an awareness of being part of the world, "God bless America" is an expression of faith in a God too small to be worthy of worship. To ask God to bless America and the world is to admit that God does not belong to us and that we are not the only people who belong to God.

This is the heart of the struggle between fundamentalist and liberal Christians. Bigger Christianity is not unpatriotic, but it does recognize the inherent dangers in an alliance between faith and patriotism. Fundamentalism does not. It has hitched its wagon to American triumphalism. It believes the only true faith is inextricably tied to America's being the greatest nation on earth. The one becomes verification of the other. Thus, when America is under attack, Christianity must come to its defense. When bad things, such as 9/11, happen to the nation, they are seen as a wake-up call for the nation to renew its ties to Christianity. When America defeats an enemy, it is a sign that God's blessings have been bestowed on a grateful people. From this perspective, national policies and priorities are evaluated on the basis of how they serve this alliance between faith and patriotism.

This way of thinking is difficult to comprehend, given the words of Jesus, "Love your enemies, do good to those who hate you, bless those who curse you, pray for those who abuse you" (Luke 6:27–28). Liberal Christians have no expectation that our national government will think or act in ways consistent with Jesus' words. But we do expect faithfulness of ourselves in trying to live by the higher calling they describe. If God blesses one nation, God blesses all. For this reason, Bigger Christianity believes American Christians should never ask God to bless our nation without also petitioning on behalf of the entire world.

Causes vs. Enemies

Implicit in everything we have said thus far in distinguishing Bigger Christianity from fundamentalism is the stark contrast in the mindset of each group.

For liberals, Bigger Christianity calls for engagement in just causes. Everything we work for—peace, all forms of justice seeking, diversity, the value of common sense, opposing the marriage amendment and environmental pollution—is to us a just cause. This is where the struggle begins and ends from the perspective of Bigger Christianity. We believe we offer a different and more biblically faithful understanding of the Christian tradition. We believe our priorities are straight and our vision of what it means to follow Jesus is clear. But this commitment to champion certain causes does not lead us to think of fundamentalists as our enemies. We see them, rather, as Christians whose views of faith, justice, and morality differ from our own in substantive ways.

Fundamentalists, on the other hand, usually speak and act from a very different perspective. Theirs is not a struggle against liberalism. It is against liberals. They are not championing a cause. They are engaged in a holy war with what they believe is an identifiable *enemy*. Rather than understanding disagreement as the clash of different causes, they see themselves as confronting an enemy that must be destroyed. They personify issues. Their words sound as if they are on a modern-day crusade to drive liberals from the land. "Convert or be banished" seems to be their battle cry.

The decline in the spirit of respectful public debate in this country coincides with the rise of fundamentalism's influence in politics. Liberal Christians do not believe this relationship is casual. We believe it is causal. Fundamentalist leaders write and speak as if they have been called by God to save the nation from the infidel liberals who are bent on destroying its moral fiber. Some of them have expanded their crusade to include leaders of other nations; Pat Robertson called for the assassination of Venezuelan President Hugo Chavez during the August 23, 2005, broadcast of his *700 Club* television show. This statement does not reflect the sentiments of all fundamentalists, to be sure, but it is a telling example of the extremes to which blind ideology can lead. When the opposition is an "enemy," it is easy to think killing is a just means to a greater end.

While liberal Christians accept fundamentalists as Christians—something they are often reluctant to do for us—we are clearly disturbed by the kind of Christians they are. Fred Phelps, a fundamentalist minister from Topeka, Kansas, is on a nationwide campaign against homosexuality because, he says, "God hates fags." He and members of his congregation frequently hold protests at the funerals of soldiers killed in Iraq. They believe the war is God's punishment of America for tolerating gays and lesbians. Liberal Christians are willing to acknowledge that Phelps and his followers are Christians. But we are also quick to add that they are not the kind of Christians we ever want to be.

The distinction between supporting a cause and turning those who disagree with you into enemies is a primary difference between Christian fundamentalism in this country and the Bigger Christianity this book advocates. It is not a small difference. The incivility surrounding controversial issues our nation is facing has more than one cause, but it is unlikely to be purged from public debate unless and until Americans reject the kind of personal attack that characterizes fundamentalism.

During the Viet Nam War some liberal Christians made the mistake of turning American soldiers into enemies, rather than remaining focused on the cause of peace. This tragic mistake led to insults being hurled at them as they returned from the battlefield, adding to the trauma to which they had already been subjected. One of the lasting lessons of Viet Nam for all Christians should be that while causes create sharp differences, they should not make us into enemies. When they do, the "war" has already been lost by both sides. An "enemy" mindset is too small to reflect the life and teachings of Jesus. Christianity can be bigger than this. Christians should be people who can champion causes while remaining respectful of those whose views challenge our own. The world and the faith we represent will be better for it if we are.

Chapter 6

Bigger Christianity and the State

*I*t was a devastating blow to Christianity." This was how former Alabama state Supreme Court Judge Roy Moore described the 2003 U.S. Supreme Court ruling against his placement of a one-ton piece of granite with the Ten Commandments chiseled on it in the rotunda of the state judicial building. He was being interviewed by Chris Matthews on his June 28, 2005, television political talk show *Hardball,* broadcast from Two Rivers Baptist Church in Nashville, Tennessee. The subject was the role of religion in American politics. The court said that such displays are constitutional only as an expression of American heritage devoid of religious intention or reference. Judge Moore interpreted this to mean displays were permissible as long as Christians didn't believe in them. That, of course, was not what the ruling said, but Judge Moore and several other Christian fundamentalist guests on the same program remained adamant about how they understood it.

At one point, Matthews asked Bobbie Patray, president of the Tennessee Eagle Forum, if it would be acceptable to her for a Buddha to be displayed in a school room. She responded, "No. That's not what our law—that's not what our country is founded on." She was referring to what she had earlier called our "Judeo-Christian heritage." But if you listen to what fundamentalist Christians actually say, there is little doubt they are talking about Christianity only. Moreover, they make some astounding assertions in the process. When Matthews asked Patray why she was upset about the court ruling on the Ten Commandments, she replied, "The Ten Commandments are the Ten Commandments. And they're the basis for our law in our country and played a huge role in the founding documents and the way that the founders thought about our country."

Is there genuine evidence the Ten Commandments were the basis for our law in this country? The Constitution makes no reference to the Ten Commandments. The Bill of Rights does not, nor the Declaration of Independence.

What our founding documents do reference is that rights and privileges such as life, liberty, and the pursuit of happiness ultimately have their roots in a benevolent Creator. They could have easily been overt in religious language and deliberate in showing preference to Christianity. It is significant that they chose not to. Fundamentalists continue to ignore this. They also ignore the fact that the Ten Commandments are not "Christian." They are part of the Torah law. Jesus quoted some of the law in the Sermon on the Mount, but he made the demands more exacting (Matthew 5:21–48). Based on what he said, a list of truly "Christian" commandments might read something like this:

> You shall not get angry with your brother or sister.
> You shall not have lust in your heart.
> You shall not get divorced.
> You shall not swear.
> You shall not resist evildoers.
> You shall not hate your enemies.

If we want the courts to allow commandments to be posted on government property, perhaps these "Christian" commandments should be. Since Islam stands in the Abrahamic tradition, perhaps some of the commands in the Qur'an should be posted. Where do displays begin and end? The court ruling did not give a definitive answer. Christian fundamentalist groups have already announced their intention to try to display other symbols of the Ten Commandments across the country. Maybe other faiths will seek to do the same thing.

The practical problems related to blurring church and state lines alone would be enough to overwhelm our court system. Instead of focusing on displays, the Christian Right might do better by heeding the advice of a letter writer to the *Minneapolis Star Tribune* who wrote:

> So, lots of people want to display the Ten Commandments in public. Instead, I'd like to see people *obey* the Ten Commandments.
>
> Let's start with No. 3, proscribing the taking of God's name in vain. We'll ban "Oh, my god!" from general speech. We'll also ban TV preachers and politicians who use God's name in search of power and riches.
>
> On to No. 4, remembering the Sabbath day and keeping it holy. That shuts down Sunday businesses and guarantees everyone will spend the day worshiping in church and resting with their families.
>
> How about No. 6, "You shall not kill." Wonderful! No more capital punishment, no more guns, no more war.
>
> No. 9's proscription against bearing false witness against your neighbor would quiet the Swift Boat Veterans and their ilk.

Finally, if we observe No. 10's ban on covetousness, we'll have to stop all advertising, which by its very nature is designed to make people covet things they don't have.[1]

This fight for Christian displays on public property wins little sympathy from non-Christians. Islamic author Reza Aslan,[2] also a panelist on the *Hard-ball* broadcast, commented after hearing the fundamentalist complaints, "I think that most Americans would be shocked to think that somehow Christianity is under attack in this country. Christians are doing just fine." Southern Baptist leader Richard Land retorted, "I think that Christians are probably better judges of whether they're being discriminated against and persecuted than people who aren't Christians."

This is how the evening went, leaving little question that what fundamentalists want is to go back to the 1950s and the age of Christian hegemony. When Chris Matthews asked the Reverend Jerry Sutton, pastor of Two Rivers Baptist Church, if our nation should go back to the time when the Bible was read and Christian prayers were recited in public schools, he answered, "If I had my way, we would." He spoke for the crowd gathered, who applauded when he finished. Fundamentalism looks back.

But our future does not lie in our past. We are not the same nation we were in the 1950s, and certainly not the nation that was founded in 1776. This is a point about which we as a people must be clear. The principles on which the nation was founded are enduring, but determining their meaning for our country that is part of a small and flat world means interpreting them as we go. That is how it has to be. When it comes to constitutional law, "strict constructionists" are the equivalent of biblical literalists. That may explain why fundamentalists like them. Not interpreting the Constitution is as impossible as not interpreting the Bible. Literalists, whether constitutional or biblical, engage in interpretation. They just don't admit it.

Separation of church and state was from the beginning a practical means of protecting the nation's democracy against Christian dominion. Our founders and their ancestors had seen and experienced it in Europe. They were determined to avoid it here. But the institutional safeguards they established do not seem to dissuade fundamentalist Christians from trying to use Christianity's majority status to impose their version of faith on others. Grounded in a belief system that divides people into the "saved" and the "lost," politics has become a *tool for evangelism*. Through this lens, democracy offers the freedom to evangelize the unconverted. For fundamentalist Christians, political issues are more than moral pronouncements. They are the means of advancing the cause of Christ on earth. Not to seek to enact legislation that is consistent with the commission to "make disciples of all nations" (Matthew 28:19) is for them an act of disobedience. The importance of this evangelistic imperative as the driving force behind the political efforts of fundamentalist Christians, that is, the Christian Right, cannot be overstated. Their zeal on issues such as abortion and homosexuality cannot be understood apart from it.

Bigger Christianity is also committed to evangelism, but in a very different way. It seeks to live its faith by balancing faithfulness to our core convictions (chapter 4) with respect for the views of others, and to let that be our witness of faith. We do not believe the laws of the land should be tools for Christian evangelizing. Rather, they should reflect universal values people of all faiths—or no faith at all—can affirm. This is what our founders sought to embody in the Constitution. These universal values ought also to serve as guides for interpreting the Constitution today.

The evangelistic zeal of Christian fundamentalists is easily overlooked in discussions about church and state, as in the case of *Divided by God: America's Church-State Problem—and What We Should Do about It* by Noah Feldman, a professor at the New York University School of Law and fellow at the New America Foundation. Before its publication, the July 3, 2005, *New York Times Magazine* ran an excerpt from the book in which Feldman summarized the solution he believes can bridge the divide. His analysis of the current conflict is compelling, but the solution misses the mark by ignoring the impact fundamentalism's evangelistic zeal will have on any effort to find a middle ground.

Before 1776, he reminds us, the history of church and state was simple. The religion of the state was whatever the religion of the ruler was. But the United States Constitution gave birth to a different way of thinking about state and religion. In a nation where the people were sovereign, he said, "the sovereign people would actively believe in religion instead of cynically manipulating it, and elite skeptics would no longer be whispering in the ears of power. Religion would be a genuinely popular, even thriving, political force."

This model called for a new understanding of church and state, and the framers of the American Constitution rose to the occasion. They designed a national government that, for the first time in Western history, had no established religion at all. The Articles of Confederation, which were drawn up during the Revolutionary War, had been silent on religion—itself something of an innovation. But the Constitution went further by prohibiting any religious test for holding office. And the first words of the First Amendment stated that "Congress shall make no law respecting an establishment of religion, or prohibiting the free exercise thereof." If the people were to be sovereign, and belonged to different religions, there would be no official, state-supported religion at all. Otherwise, the reasoning went, too many religious denominations would be in competition to make theirs the official choice, and none could prevail without coercing dissenters to support a church other than their own—a violation of the liberty of conscience that Americans had come to believe was a God-given right. Establishment of religion at the national level was prohibited. Religious diversity had ensured it. The experiment had begun.

As with all great experiments, the model has had numerous challenges that it has managed with modest success. The root of these difficulties, Feldman argues, has been "fresh infusions of religious diversity into American life have brought with them original ideas about church and state—new answers to the challenge of preserving the unity of the sovereign people in the face of their flourishing spiritual variety and often conflicting religious needs." One of the most trying challenges has been the 1971 Supreme Court ruling known as the "Lemon test," based on the case of *Lemon v. Kurtzman* in which the Court decided that a Rhode Island law allowing government payment of part of the salary of some parochial school teachers was unconstitutional. The ruling required all government decisions to be motivated by a secular purpose, but in the process of rendering this decision the court also prohibited the common practice of sanctioned prayer and Bible reading in public schools.

Two factions have developed in response to this landmark decision. On one side are what Feldman calls "legal secularists" who insist the establishment clause in the First Amendment created an impenetrable "wall of separation" that prevents any government action or passivity that can be interpreted as promoting religion. This group views religion as "a matter of personal belief and choice largely irrelevant to government." Moreover, it believes values derived from religion will divide the nation rather than unite it. On the other side are those he calls "values evangelicals." They believe there is a broad consensus among the majority of Americans on the values and principles that arise from and in respect of the religious influences present when the nation was founded.

The problem these divergent points of view raise is immediately apparent. Because of the relative success of "legal secularists" in court cases, "values evangelicals" believe that the rightful place of the nation's religious heritage has been denied by the courts in contradiction of the views of the majority of Americans. "Legal secularists" reply that the consensus on values and principles evangelicals believe exists is imagined rather than real. Thus, the appropriate role of government is to be neutral to the extent it has to be to prevent any blurring of the line between church and state.

In spite of these serious differences, Feldman believes both sides essentially want the same thing—to maintain national unity amid religious diversity. For this reason, he believes a "common ground" solution is possible. His proposal is as follows:

> The state may neither coerce anyone in matters of religion nor expend its resources so as to support religious institutions and practices, whether generic or particular. These constitutional principles, reduced to their core, can be captured in a simple slogan: no coercion and no money.

In practice, no coercion would allow religious symbols, displays, and activities in the public domain so long as there is no coercion to elicit either agreement or participation. No money would mean that no government funding in any form would be appropriated to groups and institutions in support of religious programs and activities, including faith-based programs and school vouchers for religious instruction. Feldman offers this rationale for his proposal:

> The solution I have in mind rests on the basic principle of protecting the liberty of conscience. So long as all citizens have the same right to speak and act free of coercion, no adult should feel threatened or excluded by the symbolic or political speech of others, however much he may disagree with it.

Further, he argues that secularists should confront the evangelicals' arguments on their own terms rather than trying to stop the conversation by seeking court ruling against any and all religious expressions in the public domain, as they have done in the last forty years. Argue for "the rightness of their beliefs about their own values" is his counsel to secularists. But what hope is there in such an approach? Feldman's answer is:

> Reason can in fact engage revelation, as it has throughout the history of philosophy. The skeptic can challenge the believer to explain how he derives his views from Scripture and why the view he ascribes to God is morally attractive—questions that most believers consider profoundly important and perfectly relevant.

On the face of it, the case he makes is persuasive. Both sides have to give up some things in order to reach a middle ground that creates public policy that accommodates religion without endorsing any particular tradition. But it will be a hard sell to convince secularists that minority rights should be determined by majority vote, as he suggests. After all, more than 80 percent of Americans claim to be Christian, the most zealous among them being fundamentalists. Essentially he is proposing that respect for minority rights should depend on the benevolence of the majority. This has not worked at any point in history, and our own history leaves no doubt that the majority has been less than charitable toward minorities.

But the major flaw in his two-part solution is his failure to account for the fact that fundamentalists are biblical literalists who believe nonliteralists and non-Christians are enemies to be conquered or destroyed. Inextricably bound to their worldview is an evangelistic zeal that stirs them to blur the lines separating church and state. Feldman uses the term "evangelicals" in the article as if evangelicals and fundamentalists are one and the same. This is a serious oversight. Some evangelicals are fundamentalists, but not all by any stretch. Nonfundamentalist evangelicals seldom take an "us vs. them" attitude toward liberal Christians or non-Christians. Their evangelism comes more in the form of witness rather than the subtle and often overt coercion that characterizes the zeal of fundamentalists. Fundamentalists, on the other hand, hold to the view that it's "my way or the highway." A minister of a large fundamentalist church was interviewed in 2004 by a *Lakeville Sun-Current* newspaper reporter about his church raising funds to move a Ten Commandments monument from the courthouse in Duluth, Minnesota, to a nearby park. A court order had been issued against the city allowing the monument to remain. This is how the interview went.

Reporter: Why did you get involved in the Duluth case? Why was it important?

Minister: The liberal forces behind removing the Ten Commandments were trying to muscle the display away and I thought that was wrong because in America the history has made the Ten Commandments part of our culture and identity. Someone should stand up, and the congregation joined me as we raised the money to give it back to Duluth and let it be placed in Canal Park. What stirred me up was their trying to invade our culture for something as simple as the Ten Commandments.

His language may be a bit rough around the edges, but his point is plain enough. "Liberals" are "invaders" of "our" (meaning Christian) "culture."

There is no room for compromise in this kind of attitude when it comes to church and state. Feldman believes the religious meaning of displays should be brought back into the public domain, rather than forcing people of faith to use euphemistic language to justify their efforts. But such a move would likely fuel the flames of evangelistic zeal. Only fundamentalist Christians are seeking to have displays on public property and put prayer in public schools. Feldman de facto dismisses the significance of this evangelistic zeal by asserting that "it is an interpretive choice to feel excluded by other people's faiths" when no coercion is involved. The devil is in the details—in this instance, how you define "coercion." Fundamentalist Christians do not believe open solicitation employed as a tool of evangelism is coercion. They believe a person always has the freedom to say no. Feldman acknowledges that no agreement will accommodate all people, but he believes his solution will include the largest majority possible. Apparently he is unconcerned that the minority might very well face harassment from fundamentalists who are passionate about converting them to Christianity. We need look no further than the overt Christian evangelism recently uncovered at the U.S. Air Force Academy to see how real this danger is.

After complaints that such evangelistic actions were taking place became public, an Air Force task force issued a report claiming that while it found "perceptions" of religious intolerance at the academy, there was no evidence of widespread discrimination. Academy Lutheran Chaplain MeLinda Morton called the report a whitewash. Soon thereafter she resigned her commission when told she was being reassigned to Okinawa. She later commented: "The [academy] superintendent offered me a [five-week] position on his staff, [but] the way in which the position was offered indicated they weren't serious about [religious freedom]. He expected certain loyalties."[3]

This story not only graphically illustrates the flaw in Feldman's thesis; it underscores the marked contrast in the way Bigger Christianity and fundamentalism approach the public square. The former respects religious boundaries. The latter believes none should exist. This is why liberal Christians and non-Christians agree, "It's dominion, stupid," when it comes to fundamentalism's agenda. Domination rather than accommodation is their goal. That is why Bigger Christianity believes in an impenetrable wall of separation between church and state.

This separation benefits the church as much as the nation, another point Feldman misses. As history has shown, the church has nothing to gain and much to lose by state accommodation. Freedom to worship is a value not to be taken for granted, but it is not essential for the survival of the Christian message. Ancient Israel's faith survived Babylonian captivity, though the nation did not. The Christian community thrived during persecution by the Roman Empire. James Madison recognized the advantage to the church in being independent of the state, choosing to join Thomas Jefferson in enacting the Virginia statute of religious freedom that became the basis for the establishment clause. Both men understood that Christianity is not advanced and the state does not benefit from church and state entanglement.

Bigger Christianity wonders what fundamentalists believe will be gained by their resistance to strict separation of church and state. Those of us who lived through a time when Christianity had its way in the public square do not have a sense that anything significant has been lost by this no longer being the case. More important is the obligation of people of faith to honor the link between truth and freedom on a personal basis. Jesus told the disciples that if they continued to follow him, they would know the truth and the truth would set them free (John 8:32). He was speaking about his truth, but his words certainly apply to all truth. Freedom needs truth for meaning. Without truth, freedom is always in jeopardy. The conflict over church and state is an issue about freedom, but it is also about truth. This means history cannot be rewritten to suit an agenda.

In an ironic twist, fundamentalists who say they are committed to the truth often argue in ways that make all truth opinion and all opinion truth. On the edition of *Hardball* previously mentioned, Chris Matthews asked an unidentified member of the audience about the Terri Schiavo case: "Were you surprised to hear that the diagnosis, that the autopsy showed that her brain had shriveled to half its size and that she was truly—I hate to use the term—in that vegetative state?" The man answered, "That's up to God to determine whether we're in a vegetative state or not. I can't determine that," dismissing a medical autopsy as a "human opinion."

In a world where all opinions are equal and evidence in favor of one over another is dismissed, fundamentalists can say this is a Christian nation, in open denial of historical reality. The fact that our founders chose not to establish a Christian theocracy, even though many of them were Christian, is itself a reliable basis for believing it was their clear intention not to do so.

To say, therefore, that this is a Christian nation flies in the face of what we know about actual events. Truth cannot simply be in the eye of the beholder. What is known is known until information comes along that alters it. That is quite different from saying what we know is only an opinion. Stephen Hawking suggested there was such a thing as black holes in the universe. Many facts supported his hypothesis before he established black holes themselves as fact. Even though we are still learning about the nature of black holes, Hawking's initial hypothesis was based on scientific data that gave it credibility beyond mere opinion. Intellectual integrity requires that factors pointing to one conclusion not be dismissed solely because you have reached a different one. You may think Tiger Woods is the greatest golfer of all time. You have a right to your opinion, even if someone else believes Jack Nicklaus is. What is not an opinion, though it has never been established as a fact, is that both of them play golf better than I ever have or ever will.

Liberal Christians believe dominion over the secular order was an inappropriate aim of Christianity in the past and remains so today. It is also brings no lasting advantage to faith. The founders were obviously aware of the dangers of dominion of Christianity over the state. They framed church and state relations in the Constitution not only to prevent it, but to provide for protection of Christianity from the state. What is truly ironic is that while most Americans easily recognize the dangers of a theocracy, fundamentalist Christians do not seem to appreciate the danger accommodation from the state poses to Christianity. Part of the reason may be their persistence in romanticizing American democracy to the point of ignoring its hubris, greed, and desire to make the world a reflection of itself. When Christians are quick to give their government the benefit of the doubt, they are easily manipulated for propaganda purposes.

Fundamentalism's strong support of the Bush administration on the basis that the president is a "born again" Christian is an example of what we are talking about. They have allowed themselves to become major supporters for the administration's policies that justify the nation acting like a benevolent empire in its efforts to spread democracy in the Middle East and around the world.[4] What they apparently do not see or, if they do, will not believe, is that government is not a friend of faith. The only thing Christianity needs from the government is the freedom to worship. Beyond that lies an entanglement that will shortchange Christianity every time, because government never does anything that will not advance its agenda. With government as a friend, Christianity does not need enemies. Nor does any other religious tradition. In fact, all religions have a stake in opposing the efforts of Christian fundamentalists to blur the lines between church and state. The challenge facing religious life in America today does not come from the state. It comes from a form of Christianity that wants favors from the state. Liberal Christians cannot stand alone in seeking to counter the influence of this view of church and state relations. What is needed is the establishment of a true Religious Left that will promote democracy over Christian dominion. This need is the subject of the next chapter.

Chapter 7

Bigger Christianity and a *Real* Religious Left

*T*here is a need for the formation of a *real* Religious Left, as opposed to the imaginary one that now exists in some people's minds. There is no religious left, because there are no groups of liberal Christians seeking to make the government an instrument of their moral agenda.[1] There is no religious right either, because there is no other religious tradition working to establish a theocracy in its own image except the Christian Right.

The fact that no religious right or left exists makes you wonder why someone like Jim Wallis would continue to write and speak as if there was. Wallis is senior editor of *Sojourners,* an evangelical Christian magazine that during the 2004 presidential campaign launched a nationwide campaign against making God a Republican or a Democrat. Wallis correctly recognizes that the Christian Right has hijacked the Christian faith for political purposes. Unfortunately, though, he convolutes the problem by using the phrase "religious right" and then creating a fictional counter group he identifies as "the religious left." Thus his book *God's Politics* carries the subtitle "Why the Right Gets It Wrong and the Left Doesn't Get It." But he is not alone. A recent article in the *Washington Post* was entitled "Religious Right, Left Meet in Middle: Clergy Aim to Show that Faith Unifies."[2] Even the exceptional work of Robert Wuthnow reflects the confusing interchange of "religious right" and the Christian Right, or "the New Christian Right" as Wuthnow calls it.[3]

The use of misleading labels supports the impression Christian fundamentalists try to perpetuate that all they want is to exercise their rights as citizens, just like everyone else. But they want more than this. As we suggested in the previous chapter, they want to elect officials at every level who will disregard the mandate of freedom *of* and freedom *from* religion that the Constitution guarantees. Thus, in today's America, the use of misleading labels by prominent Christian voices is not an inconsequential problem.

Liberal Christians now have a unique opportunity to build something the world has never known before—a coalition of various traditions into what can be regarded as a *real* Religious Left, a religious political force that believes faith in the public square is appropriate because it affirms universal values that undergird life, liberty, and the pursuit of happiness for *all*, not just the majority. A Religious Left of this kind could be groundbreaking. It would signal the emergence of a Christianity that accepts the truth that it is not the only pathway to God and wants to join with other faiths to work toward goals that will make the world more just and peaceful.

Because Christianity is the majority faith in this country, liberal Christians believe they should be big enough to lead the way in forming this Religious Left. In *What's Wrong with the Christian Right*, I suggested some general principles of faith called "The Liberal Christian's Manifesto." A few of them could easily be affirmed by different religious traditions and could, therefore, serve as a basis or platform of sorts on which a true Religious Left could be founded:

> We believe that being God's people doesn't mean we are the only people of God.
> We believe sacred texts are a moral guide rather than a book of rules.[4]
> We believe in life *before* death as well as after.
> We believe the many forms of diversity among people are to be celebrated rather than feared.
> We believe God blesses other nations as well as America.
> We believe in telling all the truth we know without claiming to know all the truth there is.

These affirmations are not set in stone, but they do seem to level the playing field, so to speak, among various faiths as statements of values and beliefs that transcend particularities. Common ground is the first requirement for establishing a religious voice in the public arena that rejects sectarianism. The bond holding this "coalition of the willing" together is the religious pluralism our democracy has grown into over the last 250 years. Our country does not need a counterbalance to the attitude of Christian fundamentalism in regard to church and state. It needs an *alternative*. That is what a true Religious Left would be—a movement of people of faith joined to ensure that no faith is left behind or left out as our nation moves into the twenty-first century, and that people of no faith would not fear that their freedom was being jeopardized by religious zealots. Even more, it is more than a play on words to suggest that this kind of Religious Left would actually form a religious "center." In fact, it is not too far-fetched to imagine that such a movement could become a home for conservatives, moderates, and liberals in various traditions working together to save freedom of and from religion in America.

But creating such a movement will require a new way of thinking about the link between the founding of this nation in the eighteenth century and the America of the twenty-first century, where the world is flat. At one point in the *Hardball* show from Nashville, Chris Matthews challenged liberal minister Albert Pennybacker of the Clergy and Leadership Network, "In other words, we have changed our values since Philadelphia in 1776?" Pennybacker replied, "No. We've not changed our values. We've begun to understand that we are a religiously diverse country and that we have different understandings of the nature of God and we can't inflict this on each other."

I beg to disagree with my friend Albert. I believe we as a people have changed some of our values as we have grown into a more diverse and tolerant culture. This is not the same country it was in 1776, even as the round world of the eighteenth century has become the flat world of the twenty-first century. The Declaration of Independence speaks of humanity possessing certain inalienable rights, among them life, liberty, and the pursuit of happiness. But when Mr. Jefferson penned those words, he was thinking of "whites" and "men" only. It did not occur to him that he was leaving out the black slaves he owned or the women who bore his children. Thank God we have changed values in regard to race and gender in this country.

The same can be said of religion. The founders who were religious were mostly Christian or Deistic. They were not Jewish, Muslim, Hindu, Buddhist, Taoist. But, again, thank God as a people we have changed the value we place on non-Christian traditions. Of course this nation has changed. To suggest our values have not kept pace with the social and religious changes that have taken place is to argue for living in a past that does not fit the world of today. At the same time, given the forward-looking insights our founders had, it is likely they would interpret these changes as a positive outgrowth of what they set in motion.

A better America has emerged in the last 250 years, even though individually each of us is inflicted with the same human frailties that beset our nation's founders. We are not better people than they were, but we have become a better country, thanks to countless leaders who responded boldly to the challenges of their time in history, as did our founders. They saw the sin of racism and fought to overcome it. They saw the economic injustice of a capitalism that made the rich richer and poor poorer and developed a progressive tax system to overcome it, even as they sought fair wages and safe working conditions for ordinary people. To see the ways we are a better nation than we were 50, 100, or 250 years ago speaks of the spirit of a people who want freedom and justice for all to be real, not imaginary.

Once this common ground is established, a Religious Left as I am defining it would need to begin to build genuine respect for each of the participating traditions. I want to suggest a way of doing this that is modeled after the Truth and Reconciliation Commission of South Africa. On the face of it, this may seem unorthodox, if not out of character with what is needed. But consider the work of the commission.

The TRC was established by the Promotion of National Unity and Reconciliation Act, No. 34 of 1995, soon after the election of Nelson Mandela as South Africa's new and first black president. The mandate of the commission was to bear witness to, record, and, in some cases, grant amnesty to the perpetrators of crimes relating to human rights violations, reparation, and rehabilitation. It functioned not unlike a court. Anybody who felt he or she had been a victim of violence could come forward and be heard at the TRC. Perpetrators of violence could also give testimony and request amnesty from prosecution, so long as two conditions were met: (1) the crimes were politically motivated, and (2) the entire truth was told by the person seeking amnesty.

The hearings were national and international news, and many sessions were televised on national TV. The TRC is believed to have been a crucial component of the transition to full and free democracy in South Africa and, despite its flaws, is generally regarded as having achieved its stated purpose. A total of 21,800 victims' stories were heard by the commission. Of the 7,112 requests for amnesty, 849 were granted, 5,392 were refused, and the remainder were withdrawn.

The hearings took place with victims and perpetrators hearing each other's testimonies. Everything was in the open. No closed-door or secret sessions were held. This openness that brought victims and perpetrators together may have been the key to the reconciling power of truth telling that occurred throughout South Africa. It also stands in marked contrast to the frequent practice of commissions and panels and investigations in other nations to work behind closed doors.

It would seem that the South African model would serve the interests of establishing a genuine Religious Left whose work depends on the forming of trust relationships between the religions it is seeking to bring together. The process would be for each group to hear how its beliefs and actions have impacted and are impacting all the others. At the same time, each group would have the opportunity to articulate how its beliefs and practices can contribute to reconciliation in a religiously plural America. The few groups and gatherings that have tried to bridge interfaith barriers have seldom begun with the elemental task of educating participants on the details of each tradition and the impact each has felt from the beliefs and practices of the others. As a majority faith, this process could prove to be painful to Christians. Majorities tend to impact minorities in ways the majority is unaware of. But the truth is freeing and holds the potential for reconciliation, when that is its stated goal.

The success of the South African Truth and Reconciliation Commission points to a failure of American whites and blacks to achieve a similar result in the aftermath of the civil rights conflict of the 1960s. Race relations in this country have improved, but the wounds still run deep for African Americans, perhaps because they have not had the opportunity on any large or official scale to tell their stories. It's as if the nation wants to bury the past rather than be healed through balancing truth and reconciliation. Nations are not so different from individuals in the need for trauma to be openly confronted. But race is not the only source of conflicts among Americans. Religious differences have often become a source of division, as the current cultural wars make clear. A Religious Left can be a coalition of various traditions that is willing to admit to these conflicts. In an ironic way, this level of openness has the potential of building unity by affirming the real differences that exist in a religiously plural and religiously neutral America of today. When differences are minimized, only an appearance of unity emerges. Exposing the way one faith is a sword to another can alter how those differences are perceived and expressed.

The point of suggesting a "truth and reconciliation" model be used to build the kind of Religious Left needed is that in today's world, building interfaith relationships has eclipsed the urgency that once existed in ecumenical relations. The new religious America is one in which lines that divide members of the same religious tradition are creating points of commonality between different faith traditions. Liberal Christians may now have more in common with liberal Jews and Muslims, Buddhists and Hindus, than with fundamentalist Christians. This is not to suggest efforts to reconcile internal divisions be abandoned, only to point to a new religious reality that begs for attention. The world is too small for religious conflicts to continue. More than dialogue by people of goodwill on all sides is needed to end them. Encounters at a level deeper than most of us have experienced holds the key to building bridges of truth and reconciliation over which all people of faith can travel to lands flowing with respect and affirmation of one another as the people of God.

The hope for an interfaith coalition that can sustain a new and genuine Religious Left lies at the heart of the agenda for Bigger Christianity in today's America. Thinking people of faith are weary of religions being the source of conflict around the world. In a recent "Ask the Pastor" sermon time in our congregation, when congregational members are invited to ask any faith question of their choosing, Wally asked, "Do you have any hope that the world's religions can get together in a way that will stop them from being the source of so much conflict?" My response was yes. The folly of the current fundamentalist extremism in all three Abrahamic faiths, I continued, would eventually become so obvious that it will have a moderating effect on reasonable people in all three traditions. That moderating effect will be an opportunity for members at the local level to begin exploring ways to build greater understanding and cooperation on a host of issues and problems shared by all of us. Discrimination, poverty, unjust working conditions, freedom of and freedom from religion—these are not single faith concerns. What we may not achieve working alone might well happen through interfaith efforts. Moreover, the message this cooperation would represent is that people of faith can show respect amid differences and unite resources for common causes related to justice and mercy.

This is the kind of Religious Left needed in today's America. It cannot happen, however, until Christianity becomes big enough to abandon its hegemony and to accept the validity of minority faiths in this country. A Christianity this big will understand that the gospel of Jesus Christ is spread every time a person does the will of God (Matthew 7:21). In other words, every time someone acts out of love for neighbor, does justice, loves kindness, and walks humbly in the world, God is honored. As the majority faith, Bigger Christianity must be the leader in this new Religious Left. Without Christians being big enough to provide the leadership, a real Religious Left will not be possible. At the same time, the key to building this interfaith coalition will necessarily require congregational involvement. Parachurch organizations such as those mentioned in chapter 1 have a role to play in a new Religious Left, but their efforts alone will not be sufficient. There are lessons to be learned from the ecumenical efforts of the past that failed to mobilize congregational energies toward overcoming divisions within the Christian community. The stakes are too high for an interfaith movement to make the same mistakes. The future of religion in America, not to speak of the quality and kind of American influence in the world, can be influenced by a voice that is bigger than that of Christian fundamentalism being heard today.

The general challenge is clear. What remains is to fill in the blanks in terms of what Bigger Christianity might attend to as it seeks to be faithful to its own faith while building relations with people of other faiths. What is the role of a Christianity big enough to end claims that it alone has the truth or that its way is the only path to God? Many of the details will emerge on the journey, but in the next chapter we can attempt to identify some signposts that can help us know we are going in the right direction.

Chapter 8

Bigger Christianity Setting the Agenda

*T*his book began with the recognition that fundamentalism is the Christian voice setting the "moral" agenda for political discourse in the nation. The position of political candidates on issues like abortion and homosexuality has become the litmus test for their commitment to traditional American values. Issues such as ending poverty, ending an unjust war, and facing the realities of global climate change are secondary at best. That is the reality we now face.

But as Curly in the film *City Slickers* commented, "Day ain't over yet." Upon close examination, fundamentalism's armor has discernable cracks. Their claims about winning the 2004 election for George Bush were vastly overstated. Voters concerned about "family values" included Democrats as well as Republicans. Moreover, the growing entanglement of the Republican Party and the Christian Right has come under criticism by moderates such as John Danforth, mentioned in a previous chapter. It is too early, of course, to know whether or not fundamentalism's "moral" agenda for America will come to be viewed by the majority of voters as too extreme. Elections are difficult to read, making conclusions about why people vote the way they do less reliable or predictable, as Thomas Frank's *What's the Matter with Kansas?* details.

Of one thing we can be sure, however. Unlike the media, liberal Christians are finished with being sidelined by fundamentalism's dominance. More than that, while political liberals may be a minority, just who holds the majority among Protestants and Catholics is very much an open question. Despite the fact that surveys have found that as many as 40 percent of Protestants who attend church regularly call themselves "born again," no poll has shown that a majority of Protestants or Catholics identify with this label. In fact, with a majority of Christians being unchurched, that is, not attending church on a regular basis, it is reasonable to think the majority may be more liberal than the public face of Christianity would lead us to believe.

The irony of this situation, as Robert Wuthnow has noted, is that the image of minority status in the public square can offer groups a position of power as "outsiders."[1] In regard to the future of religious politics, he says, "religious groups will have more success in speaking to the public sphere as outsiders than as insiders or as groups with a mixed or divided image."[2] Even if fundamentalists do not make up the majority of Christians in America, the Christian Right's role in the Republican Party has burdened them with the image of "insiders." This makes liberal Christians "outsiders," even if in fact we are the majority of Christians.

Being an "outsider," however, as Wuthnow underscores, carries the responsibility of actually being what we are believed to be. To speak as one outside the establishment carries with it the mandate to be outside the establishment. This was, Wuthnow points out, the key to the credibility of a Mother Teresa or Martin Luther King Jr. "People will not admire, nor fundamentally respect, the prophets who hold pulpits in luxurious suburban churches, enlist Madison Avenue to raise donations, and sit in the meeting room of government agencies and large corporations."[3]

Integrity is the point Wuthnow is making, of course. Bigger Christianity cannot say one thing and do another. Earning a right to be heard once again means attending to the same concerns within Christianity to which we are challenging the nation to pay attention. In this regard, the decline of liberal Christianity may be a blessing in disguise. As the dominant Christian voice, we have allowed ourselves to become an establishment Christianity. Supported by a civil religion that reflected our political leanings, we sat where fundamentalists now sit. The challenge we face is not to regain the prominence we once enjoyed, but to build a solid base of faith and action within our communities of faith that can help us to keep our heads when all others around us are losing theirs, to paraphrase Rudyard Kipling.

This will be more difficult than we may think, primarily because liberal Christians talk about community, but are not very adept at practicing it. Freedom of thought seems to produce a radical individualism that undermines Christian community. The following is a broad generalization, but has a ring of truth to it: Fundamentalists make big church members but small Christians. Liberals makes big Christians, but small church members. In the case of the latter, we tend to participate in community so long as it doesn't impinge on our personal autonomy. When it does, we are quick to withdraw. Bigger Christianity calls liberal Christians to a deeper level of commitment to community in Christ. Radical individualism has the potential of undermining efforts to build a real Religious Left. The challenge of creating an alternative to the Christian Right requires the power and leadership of a community-based Bigger Christianity.

This makes for a special challenge to liberal Christians. Among the three Abrahamic faiths, Christianity alone is shot through with radical individualism. Jews—and to a lesser degree, Muslims—have a deeper sense of community than Christians. In general, liberal Christians value the autonomy of the individual more than being in community with others, which lies at the root of the fact that the largest percentage of unchurched Christians are liberal. It is also why as a minority public group, Bigger Christianity offers a weak alternative to fundamentalism. Without the growth in commitment to community among liberals, Bigger Christianity has little chance of having a voice strong enough to call other religious traditions to the table of religious pluralism.

From personal experience I can attest that building this commitment in liberal congregations is a very difficult task. We frequently use the word "covenant" in our faith community, but we often exhibit an insufficient intensity to give it power and presence. Bigger Christianity cannot be a formidable alternative to the small Christianity of fundamentalism without being embodied in communities of faith throughout the nation. At risk is the soul of both the nation and Christianity. Mainline congregations will need to be sanctuaries for Christians who teach and preach, talk and walk, a faith big enough to meet this challenge. In the face of declining numbers, monies, and influence, a mainline remnant exists that has yet to recognize the potential it now possesses to band together in a coalition of liberal Christians who can forge interfaith alliances to preserve the religious neutrality of the American government. But to seize the opportunity at hand, liberal Christians will have to choose community over individual autonomy.

As logical as this choice sounds, it will not be easy. One reason is that minorities and women know through experience the power of community to act in oppressive ways. But mainline churches have made significant strides forward on this front and have a deeper awareness that our future must include even greater openness to nonwhite, nonmale leadership. But none of it will translate into leadership for building a real Religious Left unless liberal Christians are willing to stay with and/or return to the church. Our pews are empty not only because fundamentalists left. They are empty because liberal Christians left before them. The return of these exiles is essential for Bigger Christianity to have sufficient inward strength to lead in interfaith coalition building.

Attracting those who have given up on the church is in truth a call to liberal communities of faith to get back to basics. This means ridding ourselves of distractions that prevent the church from being the church. In too many instances Bigger Christianity is being held hostage to a dead institutionalism that has failed to understand the foolishness of its own ways. The result is that liberal Christians are often our own worst enemy because we do not recognize the extent to which we are distracted. Christianity is not about being the church. The church is about being Christianity in the world. For this to be true, however, the church itself must be Christian. Up to now, liberal Christians have focused on not being fundamentalists more than on being bigger Christians. For this reason, it would be a serious error in self-examination to suppose that we are mature enough in faith to embody an authentic Christianity big enough for a small and flat world.

This raises the all-important question of what a mature Christian faith is. Everything we have said to this point would qualify as part of Bigger Christianity's answer. What we have not addressed in a direct way, though, is how liberal churches can function to empower their members to live out the specifics of a Bigger Christianity we have already discussed. How liberal churches function will determine whether or not Bigger Christianity becomes communalized or is left solely in the hands of individuals having to fend for themselves. As treated in the provocative work of Robert Fuller in *Spiritual, but Not Religious,* the work of Gordon Allport offers a helpful way to answer this question. Fuller has digested Allport's effort to use psychological measures for a healthy faith development in a way that makes it easily accessible for our purposes.

Allport suggested five categories for evaluating a healthy and mature faith. The first was "well differentiated." This is the ability to get beyond either/or thinking while having the capacity to judge ideas on their merit, weighing them fairly and honestly. A "well-differentiated" faith is also able to adapt and grow and learn continually through experience and study. In other words, it is flexible, not rigid. This is the kind of faith Bigger Christianity churches want their members to have. Thinking for one's self and raising questions would be encouraged as tools for achieving a "well-differentiated" faith that is consistent with Bigger Christianity's focus on journey. But Bigger Christianity churches will need to be intentional in creating an environment, if they are going to attract liberal Christians, whose image of church is one that stifles questions and opts for conformity.

The next two categories are (2) dynamic and (3) productive of a consistent morality. At issue is human initiative, over against reliance on supernatural powers. This raises an old issue, going back to the fifth-century Pelagian controversy. Pelagius, a British monk, was scandalized by what he believed was immoral living by the inhabitants of Rome when he visited the city around 390. He preached a gospel of human ability to keep the commandments if they truly desired to do so. He rejected Augustine's notion of original sin, believing instead that Adam's fall infected only Adam, not the entire human race. Thus, human will was not impaired by Adam's sin, and therefore people were responsible for their own moral actions. For his trouble—and in no small measure because of Augustine's attacks on him—Pelagius was excommunicated in 415 by Pope Innocent I. But the controversy hardly died with him. The nature of the relationship between divine grace and human effort or free will has been a continuing point of concern and controversy. Allport believed mature faith involved taking active and intentional responsibility for one's moral development and decision-making. Whatever role God plays in human activity is not in lieu of human effort. To think otherwise is to be morally irresponsible.

Bigger Christianity might be rightly described as semi-Pelagian in its focus on human efforts in moral decision making, especially as they impinge on issues of social justice. There may be times when we do what we don't want to do and don't do what we want to do (Romans 7:14-20), but that is no excuse for not doing what we know is right and ignoring instances when wrong is being done in plain view. Bigger Christianity understands that mature Christians do not talk about divine grace at the expense of the importance of human efforts, nor does the church need to fear reliance on God will be abandoned when human beings are called to be accountable for their actions and inactions.

The fourth measure of a mature faith in Allport's thinking is that it should be integral and comprehensive. Compartmentalizing one's faith leads to beliefs being so heavenly they aren't worth an earthly thing. Here the focus of faith becomes salvation. Liberal faith, on the other hand, believes in life before death. Bigger Christianity churches seek to create a community of justice and mercy on earth as a model for the way the world should function. Promises of life after death without a commitment to life in the here and now ring hollow. Moreover, as Fuller points out, comprehensiveness involves humility and tolerance, for the obvious reason that no single understanding of how God relates to our world can be fully adequate. Bigger Christianity churches will teach members to live the truth they know without needing to claim to know all the truth there is. The degree to which we are successful in this work will determine the level of maturity of faith among liberal Christians.

The final category is heuristic or open-endedness. This is the essence of faith as a journey as opposed to faith as doctrine. It is also the key to attracting open-minded Christians back to the church, and holding the ones we still have. Fuller's use of Allport's criteria for mature faith is to argue that unchurched spiritual traditions measure up against churched Christianity in quality of faith. If that is the case, it is yet another reason Bigger Christianity churches need to be forceful in presenting their approach to spiritual development in public. The message unchurched sojourners in the faith should hear from us is that there is a place for them to join with others who share their level of spiritual maturity in how we understand faith development and, thus, how we function in community with one another. Moreover, if Bigger Christianity is to become a public voice on behalf of a real Religious Left, it will have to have a level of influence in communities across the nation it once did. Without this stronger voice, non-Christians will have little reason to trust that there are many Christians who do not condemn their beliefs or support a "benevolent dictator" role for Christianity in America. Bigger Christianity can be an influence in respecting the fact that this is truly a religiously pluralistic nation that needs a religiously neutral central government.

But the task of community building among Bigger Christianity churches does not stop here. In a real sense, we have to be about faith development within our fellowships already. This involves many things, but, as Robert Wuthnow points out, none is more important than teaching our children the way we approach faith development. He believes that fundamentalism probably will continue to define the issues in the moral debate between themselves and liberals because they have done and do "a highly effective job in transmitting their beliefs to their children."[4] Bigger Christianity churches fail to do the same thing. "Will our children have faith?" is not a rhetorical question.

Early one morning last fall as Joy and I drove to our exercise class mentioned earlier, we noticed that the parking lot of a congregation of the Church of Jesus Christ of Latter-day Saints was full of cars. The next day it was the same story. We speculated that it must be a men's breakfast group meeting before work, a prayer group of some sort, or an exercise group. This went on for several weeks until one morning as we were running late we saw teenagers coming out of the building. We were shocked. The high school students we knew, not unlike our own when they were teens, "didn't do" early morning. We could not imagine what kind of church group these kids could be. A short time later we opened the Saturday morning newspaper to find a story about 900 area high school students getting up early every weekday morning during the school year to attend faith development classes at their Mormon church. Even more astounding than the early hour and the yearlong program was the fact that they did this all four years of high school.

This is not something our congregation would attempt, yet it may be that the problem is not our teenagers but the modest challenges we put to them. Whichever the case, we simply do not measure up to this kind of transmission of the faith when it comes to teaching our children what it means to live a Bigger Christianity. Teaching a liberal faith is not as easy as inculcating children and youth with dogma and doctrine, but mainline churches have not given adequate attention to this part of their ministry, opting instead for entertainment meetings and mission trip experiences, both of which have a place, but neither of which, alone or together, can impart the tradition to the next generation of bigger Christians. Yet the answer may not be as complicated as it would appear. If example is the best teacher, Bigger Christianity churches can become the kind of Christian we want our children to grow up to be.

There is ample evidence that this is precisely how children can learn and will learn the faith of their liberal parents and church family. James Fowler's *Stages of Faith* took the mainline church by storm in the early 1980s, but in most places we failed to do more than read the book. Fowler argued that all people go through the same stages of faith development, the difference between them being primarily a matter of which stage they were in. This echoed the work of thirteenth-century mystic Bernard Clairveaux, whose stages of love offer a similar measure of the stage of spiritual maturity a person might be in. In Fowler's typology, stage four is the conventional faith stage, when children acquire an understanding of faith through stories and rituals. In the process, he says, they develop feelings of emotional stability and a strong sense of communal belonging.

This is where most people stay, Fowler conjectured. Only a few individuals move to stage five, where they begin to question the authority of their church that lies behind the system of beliefs they were taught. This is the point at which they begin to develop genuine spiritual maturity, willingly taking responsibility for their own thinking and their own faith development, especially when it comes to moral questions. While this stage is a sign of solid faith development, Fowler says its weakness is that it remains in the realm of "either/or" thinking. A person believes this while rejecting that. One theological perspective cannot embrace any other. This is not so different from stage four in its rigidity, except that the person is doing the choosing rather than accepting what was taught by the community.

The most mature stage would obviously be beyond number five, where shades of gray enter into one's view. Fowler calls this the "paradoxical-consolidative" stage wherein a person of faith becomes aware of the reality of polarities in ideas and beliefs and is able to admit that no single point of view contains the whole truth. It is in this stage that one becomes most open to diversity of thought and people.

Obviously this is the stage where Bigger Christianity churches want their members to reside. But that means the churches themselves will have to model this kind of community to their children, loving and supporting them all along the stages of their development until they realize this is the place their community of faith wants them to be.

This extensive focus on Bigger Christianity becoming communalized reflects the conviction that the success of our offering an alternative to fundamentalism and helping to build a real Religious Left will depend on Bigger Christianity becoming the core faith of mainline churches. Parachurch groups such as we mentioned in chapter 1 have a role to play, but without it being congregationally based, there is not much chance that the perspectives of Bigger Christianity expressed in this book will become mainstream in the church or have a significant voice in the public square. Right-wingers, of course, accuse liberal Christians of being out of touch with ordinary Americans. In a July 1, 2005, *Wall Street Journal* commentary entitled "From Gospel to Government," Heritage Foundation fellow Joe Loconte charged that liberal Christian groups have "no obvious grassroots constituency." They are, instead, "composed mostly of mainline clergy and church elites who are often culturally out of step with the rank and file" and "treat traditional religion with either suspicion or outright contempt." As far right as Loconte is, there is at least a warning in his charge worth heeding. Liberal Christian leaders must ensure that Bigger Christianity appeals not only to those who have left the church because of its small Christianity. It can and must make its way into the minds and hearts of those Christians who have chosen to stay in mainline churches.

Wuthnow points out that much of the success of the Christian Right is attributable to Jerry Falwell being able to tap into a "preexisting network of independent Baptist clergy who could be pressed into service as state and local chairmen of the Moral Majority." These clergy were mostly congregational pastors. Therein lies a basic challenge for clergy and laity who believe in a Bigger Christianity. Wuthnow believes mainline churches have the potential for creating similar networks, such as regional and judicatory associations bringing clergy into contact with one another without a massive centralized organization being necessary. Ironically, this is where our decline may serve us in a very practical way. Wuthnow also points out that after World War II, coming on the heels of the debacle of the Scopes Monkey Trial and the Great Depression, fundamentalist Christians were sidelined in their belief system and, thus, chose to individualize their faith while staying in mainline Protestant churches. Today they have recognized the power of being together, which is why there has been an explosion of megachurches that have been successful in attracting mainline fundamentalists away from their historic church affiliations into these newly formed communities of like-minded believers.

Nevertheless, mainline churches remain a gathering place for liberals and fundamentalists, and, as such, continue to live with tensions in their effort to mature into Bigger Christianity churches. Diversity always has potential for the tyranny of the minority that is often vocal and passionate in opposing Bigger Christianity and its fruits. This means clergy and laity leadership must be bold, albeit pastoral, in confronting this tyranny. The day of passive leadership is over for Bigger Christianity churches. Fundamentalism has thrived because of strong clergy and lay leadership with a shared vision of how faith intersects with politics. It will be no different in our churches when it comes to leadership. The risks of preaching and teaching a liberal faith that makes Christianity big enough for a small world are great, but the perils of silence are so much greater. In a PriceWaterhouse television commercial worth viewing, a company executive is shown in serious thought over the future of the company. In the background a narrator is quoting from the poem "Casey at the Bat." The commercial ends with the words, "Businesses today need a Chief Courage Officer."

Bigger Christianity churches need a similar kind of courageous leadership. The issues are too serious, and the stakes regarding their outcome too high, for us to do business as usual. America needs a Christianity that is bigger than the public face on it at the moment. The world needs a Religious Left that can counter the words and actions of radical fundamentalism in all three Abrahamic traditions that fuel the fires of conflict and war. Both are possible, but neither will happen on their own. The time is now for liberal Christians to stop watching what is happening and start making new things happen in the name of the God who is bigger than all of us.

Notes

PREFACE

1. Christian fundamentalism is known today by the company it keeps. Names like Falwell, Robertson, and Dobson immediately come to mind. But in general, fundamentalists believe the Bible is the literal Word of God, thus, an inerrant and infallible moral command about how to think and act.

CHAPTER 1: A BIGGER CHRISTIANITY

1. In his subsequent autopsy report, Jon Thogmartin, medical examiner for Florida's Pinellas-Pasco County, said that Terri Schiavo had suffered from an irreversible brain injury and would not have recovered, as her parents insisted was possible.

2. Rob Stein, "Pharmacists' rights at front of new debate: Because of beliefs, some refuse to fill birth control prescriptions," *Washington Post*, March 28, 2005, A01.

3. Broadcast of *This Week* with George Stephanopoulos, May 1, 2005.

4. The brochure was also on their Web site. The telecast was aired April 25, 2005.

5. "Time Is Running Out to Strike a Blow against Judicial Tyranny," April 28, 2005, Focus on the Family Web site.

6. *The Free Presbyterian Magazine* (http://www.fpchurch.org.uk/EbBI/fpm/2005/pdf/February.pdf. "Notes and Comments: The Asian Tsunami").

7. Ian Johnston, "Tsunami was divine visitation upon 'Sabbath pleasure seekers,'" reported in *The Scotsman,* Scotland's National Newspaper Online, February 19, 2005.

8. "Hurricane Katrina Destroys New Orleans Days before 'Southern Decadence,'" an August 31, 2005, press release posted on www.repentamerica.com at www.repentamerica.com/pr_hurricanekatrina.html.

9. Jeff Sharlet, "Soldiers of Christ: Inside America's most powerful megachurch," *Harper's Magazine,* May 2005. The article was also posted on the Harper's Web site on May 26 (Harpers.org).

10. Michelle Cottle, "Let's not talk about sex. Prayer Center," *New Republic*, May 23, 2005, 21–25.

11. Robert Wuthnow, *Christianity in the 21st Century: Reflections on the Challenges Ahead* (New York: Oxford University Press, 1993), 164.

12. Thomas Friedman, *The World Is Flat: A Brief History of the Twenty-first Century* (New York: Farrar, Straus, & Giroux, 2005).

13. Ibid., 9.

14. Ibid., 10.

15. Ibid.

16. Ibid.

17. Ibid., 11.

18. Robert C. Fuller, *Spiritual but Not Religious* (New York: Oxford University Press, 2001), 5.

19. Ibid., 19, 27.

CHAPTER 2: FRAMING A BIGGER CHRISTIANITY

1. George Lakoff, *Don't Think of an Elephant! Know Your Values and Frame the Debate* (White River Junction, VT: Chelsea Green Publications, 2004), xv.

2. This was sent to me by a colleague. The author or origin of the parody is unknown to me.

3. Robert Wuthnow, *Christianity in the 21st Century* (New York: Oxford University Press, 1993), 126.

4. Ibid., 9–10.

5. John C. Danforth, "Onward Modern Christian Soldiers," *New York Times*, June 17, 2005, Op-Ed.

CHAPTER 3: BIGGER CHRISTIANITY AS A VOICE FOR GOD

1. Linda Kulman, "Religion in America: Pumping Life into Mainline Protestantism," USNews.com, posted June 6, 2005.

CHAPTER 4: BIGGER CHRISTIANITY FOR A SMALL WORLD

1. William H. Willimon and Stanley Hauerwas, *Lord, Teach Us to Pray: The Lord's Prayer and the Christian Life* (Nashville: Abingdon Press, 1996), 13–14.

2. Ibid., 15.

3. Jan Linn, *The Jesus Connection: A Christian Spirituality* (St. Louis: Chalice Press, 1997).

4. This study was done by researchers at the University of California, Berkeley, reported in UCBerkeley News online in a story entitled "Can money buy happiness?" by Carol Hyman, Media Relations, June 16, 2003. See also Peter Svensson, "Money vs. happiness: Economists find luxury purchases don't lead to contented life," Courier-Journal.com, Business, December 5, 2004.

5. Martin Wolk, "Money, is it overrated? Economic research focuses on what makes people happy," MSNBC, December 20, 2004.

6. I first encountered this term and its definition in the PBS documentary *Affluenza,* narrated by Scott Simon.

7. For a discussion of the relationship between chapter 7 and chapter 8 regarding the Jerusalem offering, see Charles Talbert, *Reading Luke* (New York: Crossroads, 1987), 181–88.

8. Rudyard Kipling, "If."

CHAPTER 5: EMBRACING BIGGER CHRISTIANITY

1. Nelson Mandela, *Long Walk to Freedom* (New York: Little, Brown & Co., 1994).

2. Eckhart Tolle, *Stillness Speaks* (Novato, CA: New World Library, 2003), 17.

3. Ibid.

4. Ibid.

5. Diana Eck, *A New Religious America: How a "Christian Country" Has Become the World's Most Religiously Diverse Nation* (San Francisco: Harper SanFrancisco, 2001), 4.

6. Ibid., 5.

7. Ibid.

8. Ibid., 36–37.

9. Ibid., 47.

10. NPR's *Morning Edition,* March 2, 2005, recounted the story of one such immigrant being so shackled in spite of the fact that he was an assistant manager of the local Country Buffet restaurant, owned a home, and was paying taxes.

11. Eck, *A New Religious America,* 47.

12. Ibid.

13. See livingthequestions.com for information about this study and how to purchase it.

14. Harold J. Rothwax, *Guilty: The Collapse of the Criminal Justice System* (New York: Random House, 1996).

15. Ibid., 12.

16. Ibid., 13.

17. Ibid., 33.

18. Ibid., 49.

19. Ibid., 32.

20. Barbara Rossing, *The Rapture Exposed* (Boulder, CO: Westview Press, 2004).

21. Ibid., 11.

22. Ibid., 46.

23. Ibid., 174.

24. Rothwax, *Guilty,* 64.

25. Ibid., 60.

26. Both definitions from the *American Heritage Desk Dictionary* (New York: Houghton Mifflin Co., 1981).

27. Ronald J. Sider, *Scandal of the Evangelical Conscience: Why Are Christians Living Just Like the Rest of the World?* (Grand Rapids: Zondervan, 2004).

28. Albert Einstein, *Out of My Later Years,* 4th ed. (Secaucus, NJ: Citadel Press, 1979), 24.

29. Ibid., 22.

30. Ibid., 5.

31. Ibid., 26.

32. Ibid., 30.

33. Mark Noll, *The Scandal of the Evangelical Mind* (Grand Rapids: Eerdmans, 1994).

34. Ibid., 7.

35. Ibid., 8.

36. Noll goes on to argue that this anti-intellectualism has cultural, institutional, and theological dimensions (12–23).

37. Noll, *Scandal,* 141.

38. Ibid.

39. *American Heritage Dictionary,* 299.

40. Reported in the *Minneapolis Star Tribune,* June 23, 2005.

41. Remarks made before the Sugarland Rotary Club in Houston, TX, March 2005, as reported in the *Fort Bend/Southwest Sun* online newspaper April 2, 2005.

42. Bob Herbert, "Cruel and Unusual," *New York Times,* Op-Ed, June 23, 2005.

43. Jean Hopfensperger, "Schiavo family unswayed by autopsy's conclusions," *Minneapolis Star Tribune,* June 17, 2005.

44. Katherine Kersten, "Profound questions from the Schiavo case," *Minneapolis Star Tribune,* June 16, 2005.

45. Agape Press online news, June 20, 2005, compiled by Jody Brown and reported by Bill Fancher.

46. Mireya Navarro, "Here Comes the Mother-to-Be," *New York Times,* March 13, 2005.

47. Reinhold Niebuhr, *Moral Man and Immoral Society* (New York: Charles Scribner's Sons, 1932), 6.

48. Cal Thomas, syndicated columnist, "Putting it in perspective," June 2, 2005.

49. Reported January 2005. http://www.aclu.org/torturefoia/release/fbi.121504.5053.pdf.

50. According to Anthony Lewis ("Guantanamo's long shadow," *New York Times,* Op-Ed, June 20, 2005), the al-Khatani story first appeared in an article in *Time* magazine June 12, 2005, based on an official log of interrogations of al-Kahtani over fifty days from November 2002 to January 2003. In an online version of an interview by Jeffrey Brown for the *Jim Lehrer News Hour,* June 13, 2005, the author of the *Time* story, Adam Zagorin, said the log "was produced on laptops, not contemporaneously, but someone would write what had happened immediately after each sort of episode. Sometimes it's hour by hour, sometimes it's minute by minute, and it would be people who were either observing or participating in the interrogation, typically uniformed military personnel, although whether they'd be wearing the uniform at the time I don't know."

51. Quoted in an MSNBC online, June 9, 2005, article entitled, "Shut down Guantanamo? U.S. eyes options."

52. Reported by the Associated Press, July 30, 2005, and picked up by truthout.org.

53. Jimmy Carter, *Our Endangered Values: America's Moral Crises* (New York: Simon and Schuster, 2005), 132–33.

54. Quoted by Bob Herbert, "Who we are," *New York Times,* Op-Ed, August 1, 2005.

55. Ibid.

56. "The Women of Gitmo," July 15, 2005.

57. Reported on truthout.org on August 5, 2005, from the original story, "Iraq's Child Prisoners," by Neil Mackay in the *Sunday Herald* of Glasgow, Scotland.

58. For a critical piece on Graham's support of American military might and American capitalism, without expressing concern for the misuse of power or economic oppression, see Jim A. Siekes, "A voice for God in places of power," *Minneapolis Star Tribune,* June 25, 2005, Op-Ed.

59. All polling in the last two weeks of June 2005 has shown that nearly 60 percent of Americans believe we should bring our troops home now.

60. Wendell Berry, "A Citizen's Response to the National Security Strategy of the United States of America," in Wendell Berry and David James Duncan, *Citizens Dissent: Security, Morality, and Leadership in an Age of Terror,* a publication of the Orion Society, 2003, 7.

61. "Veiled Praise," *New York Times,* June 23, 2005, Op-Ed.

62. Evangelicalism is distinct from fundamentalism in that it is less dogmatic and judgmental and has a long tradition of peacemaking and social outreach. At the same time, fundamentalist minister Ted Haggard, mentioned in chapter 1, is the president of the National Association of Evangelicals.

63. Excerpt from paid advertisement, *Grand Rapids Press,* May 20, 2005.

64. Advertisement, *Grand Rapids Press,* May 21, 2005.

65. Posted May 23, 2005, on www. AlbertMohler.com.

66. In "The Broken News," a speech presented by Minnesota Public Radio, May 9, 2005.

67. Wolf Blitzer Report, CNN, July 11, 2005.

68. Berry, "Citizen's Response," 7.

69. Ibid., 9.

70. Niebuhr, *Moral Man and Immoral Society,* 172.

71. Ibid., 234.

72. Ibid., 246.

73. Ibid., 247.

74. Ibid.

75. John Deutch, "Time to pull out. And not just from Iraq," *New York Times,* July 15, 2005, Op-Ed.

76. Stanley Hauerwas, *The Peaceable Kingdom* (Notre Dame, IN: University of Notre Dame Press, 1983), xvii.

77. As reported in "Cindy's Victory" by William Rivers Pitt, truthout.org/Perspective, August 15, 2005.

78. Jonathan Harr, *A Civil Action* (New York: Vintage Books, 1996).

79. Robert Fulghum, *All I Really Need to Know I Learned in Kindergarten* (New York: Random House Books, 1988).

80. This release was made on March 29, 2005, on the NRDC Web site at nrdc.org. This release also explained how the White House altered the original recommendations: "The guidelines announced today, which dictate how EPA regulates cancer-causing chemicals, finalize a draft policy issued by EPA in March 2003. That draft policy included supplemental guidelines for assessing cancer risks to children.

"The guidelines had to go through several rigorous scientific reviews before they were released today.

"EPA's draft guidelines, including the children's supplemental, first passed through an internal agency review two years ago. The agency's Scientific Advisory Board reviewed the guidelines and agreed with EPA's conclusion that early-life exposures to chemical pollutants increase cancer risk. The board recommended finalizing EPA's draft guidelines as written. The guidelines then went to the White House Office of Management and Budget (OMB) for scrutiny, where they languished until today. Out of public view, OMB substantially weakened the guidelines by adding language that will allow the chemical industry to contest policy decisions more easily, according to NRDC. Specifically, OMB inserted language allowing for 'expert elicitation,' opening the door for any outside party to challenge the way EPA applies the guidelines to assess chemicals. Such a challenge could slow the agency down for months, if not years, in making a decision on regulating a cancer-causing chemical, according to NRDC. OMB further weakened the guidelines by adding language requiring any EPA cancer evaluation to meet the standards of the Data Quality Act, a law designed by tobacco industry consultants to quash protective regulations. By opening the process to relentless industry challenges, said Dr. Sass, OMB set the bar so high that children will not be adequately protected from many cancer-causing chemicals."

81. Jeffrey Sachs, from an excerpt in *Time* magazine, March 14, 2005, from his book *The End of Poverty* (New York: Penguin, 2005).

82. Ibid., 232.

83. From the Monterrey Consensus, draft outcome of the International Conference On Financing Development, Monterrey, Mexico, March 21–22, 2002, p. 2.

84. Sachs, *End of Poverty,* 340.

85. See the stunning essay "When Compassion Becomes Dissent," by David James Duncan, in *Citizens Dissent,* 47.

86. From their Web site: mfso.org.

CHAPTER 6: BIGGER CHRISTIANITY AND THE STATE

1. The writer was Craig M. Wiester of Minneapolis, whose letter appeared on June 29, 2005.

2. Aslan is the author of *No God But God: The Origins, Evolution, and Future of Islam* (New York: Random House, 2003).

3. Quoted in *The Lutheran,* July 2005, p. 48, and posted on thelutheran.org Web site August 2005.

4. For a provocative analysis of America as an empire and the dangers this poses to Christianity, see Jack Nelson-Pallmeyer's *Saving Christianity from Empire* (New York: Continuum, 2005).

CHAPTER 7: BIGGER CHRISTIANITY AND A *REAL* RELIGIOUS LEFT

1. In July 2005, Rabbi Michael Lerner hosted a conference in Berkeley, California, he described as "spiritual Activism." The purpose of the conference was to form an alliance of "religious, secular and spiritual, but not religious, progressives." Lerner says this alliance will oppose the Christian Right's "abuse of scripture to promote war, intolerance and ugly corporate agendas," though that is not its primary objective, as reported in "The religious left fights back" by Van Jones, Alternet.org, July 28, 2005.

2. By Alan Cooperman, *Washington Post,* June 15, 2005, page A01.

3. Wuthnow interchanges these terms throughout the book, *Christianity in the 21st Century* (New York: Oxford University Press, 1993), but see especially chapter 11, "The Future of the Religious Right," 151–67.

4. Originally this said "Bible" rather than "sacred texts."

CHAPTER 8: BIGGER CHRISTIANITY SETTING THE AGENDA

1. Robert Wuthnow, *Christianity in the 21st Century: Reflections on the Challenges Ahead* (New York: Oxford University Press, 1993), 127.

2. Ibid., 176.

3. Ibid., 174.

4. Ibid., 132.